Pain, Set and Match

Bill Norris

with Richard Evans

Forward by John McEnroe

Pain, Set and Match.

Amazon books may be purchased for educational, business, or sales promotional use. For information, please e-mail Amazon books.

FIRST EDITION

Authored by Bill Norris with Richard Evans. Contributions by John McEnroe, Todd Ellenbecker and John Mark Jenkins. Photographs by Russ Adams, Susan and Fred Mullane of Camerawork USA, Art Seitz, Michael Cole, c/AFP Getty Images, Fred Sabine, Willi Schraml, Kurt Wallace. Commentaries by Andre Agassi, Mike Bryan, Pat Cash, Jim Courier, Dr. David Dines, Chris Evert, Brad Gilbert, Rafael Nadal, Andy Roddick, Larry Stefanki and Mats Wilander. Cover design and artwork by Ari Norris, Prepared for publication by Lisa Norris Stein.

Library of Congress Cataloging-in-Publishing Data has been applied for.

IBSN: 13 978-0692224120

To Sherie
You are the love of my life.

To my children
Lisa, Darren and Ari

To my grandchildren
Zoey, Beckett, Sumi and Miku

You are the world to me.

Pain, Set & Match

This is a book in two parts. Section I is Bill's stories from his life and times on the tennis circuit. Section II offers detailed instruction on prevention and recovery from injuries that are common to tennis players or athletes of any discipline.

Pain, Set & Match

A Forward by John McEnroe

Bill Norris is a one off, a real original. I have been treated by quite a few athletic trainers during my rather alarmingly long career but there has never been anyone like Bill.

I suppose, even above his technical abilities as a sports medicine therapist and healer, it was his personality that made him an indispensable part of the ATP tour – and frequently the US Davis Cup team – for over thirty years. You have to be a very special kind of person to spend your days working in a corner of a locker room for ten to twelve hours with a sweaty bunch of highly competitive, hyped-up young men who are all trying to beat each other.

The athletic trainer's training room, if he was lucky to actually have a room to himself, was never very big so you can imagine what it was like to have me and Jimmy Connors or me and Ivan Lendl – neither of whom were my best buddies to put it mildly – lying virtually side by side either before or after a big match as Bill tended to both our needs. The temperament of a saint was what was required and that was what Bill had.

Bill had been working with the ATP for more than a decade when I showed up in the late 1970's. As a teenager I was shy and never comfortable around adults I didn't know. But Bill immediately made me feel at ease and when I learned that he had worked for the Knicks and the Mets, two New York teams that I had followed as a young kid, I was impressed. This guy had worked on my idols.

The idea of having an athletic trainer give me therapy and help with little aches and pains was something quite new to me. At school and college I had just got out there and played every sport going from tennis to soccer to basketball and never thought much about how to stay fit. I just played.

But getting treatment from Bill was more than just therapy. He always had a smile on his face, always had some silly, funny line that made you laugh and helped break the tension as you got ready to go on court. Amazingly, he never got pissed, never took offense when someone came off court swearing after a loss and started complaining because he was working on someone else. The strains and stresses of having to play top class tennis in a different city; often a different country, every week are considerable but Bill just let the fall out wash over him. He relished the diversity and the camaraderie, much of which he fostered himself with that ready smile and look of wide-eyed wonder. For him the world was one big adventure and his enthusiasm was infectious. Because of Bill, the locker room became a place where I could relax which, for someone with my temperament, was no small thing!

And he made you laugh. When he wore glasses, he was a dead ringer for John Denver, a colossal Country & Folk singing star at the time, and we spent a hilarious week in Cleveland one year with Bill deliberately pretending to be Denver, signing autographs and everything.

Unlike the regular tour, team spirit is essential during Davis Cup ties and Bill played a huge part in that. Without ever appearing to be pushy, Bill always seemed to be at the heart of everything we did. When I beat Mats Wilander in a six hour marathon against Sweden in St Louis, courtside pictures went out all over the world with me celebrating with our captain, Arthur Ashe, and Bill was right there, right in the picture. It was fine by us.

As a young player, you got excited just being around our athletic trainer. He pumped you up, but more than that, his expertise in sports medicine gave you the confidence to go out and play well. Looking back on it, the most incredible thing was, he never had favorites – or if he did, you never knew. He inspired us all.

And he wasn't shy of promoting Bill Norris either. He promoted some brands of lotion that he felt were particularly effective and favored certain materials for taping injuries. He was called the Wizard of Gauze which we thought was right on the button.

Now, as I try to keep an aging body in one piece on the ATP Champions tour or Jim Courier's PowerShares Series, I always look forward to the ATP event in Delray Beach. It is driving distance from Bill's home in Boca Raton. He looks after us old guys for that week with his therapeutic treatments. But it's the smile and the silly jokes we look forward to the most.

Pain, Set & Match

Introduction

For more than forty years I lived at the epicenter of the men's tennis tour in more places than you can imagine or I can remember. I have observed, from my corner of the locker room, the great stars that have spanned four decades in all their moods. They range from jubilation bordering on euphoria, to a despair that cannot contain the tears running down their cheeks. I have seen them at the extremes of fatigue and in pain and have tried to ease that pain because that is my job. I massage egos as well as treat bodies and try to get them back on court in sufficient shape to play their best tennis. On occasion to tell them they will only be doing harm if they try.

I arrived from those other worlds of baseball and basketball to find a tour populated by fair dinkum Aussies like Rod Laver, Ken Rosewall and Fred Stolle. I watched it move through the eras of Arthur Ashe and Stan Smith; Ilie Nastase and Guillermo Vilas; Bjorn Borg, John McEnroe and Jimmy Connors. After them came the Boris Becker and Stefan Edberg period until the arrival of that great American quartet of Pete Sampras, Andre Agassi, Jim Courier and Michael Chang. And so on, to the present rivalry between a unique quartet of superstars in Roger Federer, Rafael Nadal, Novak Djokovic and Andy Murray.

A more diverse cast of characters it would be impossible to find. But partially, I suppose, because they needed me, I am privileged to say almost all of them became my friends.

For me, it was always a pleasure. I bought into the tour and the tour bought into me and the work didn't stop when the last treatment of the day was done. The job consumed me and how my wife Sherie put up with the hours I worked I shall never know.

Tennis was not how it began for me. I had gotten into sports therapy as a result of being hired as the head athletic trainer for the New York Knicks which meant I spent a lot of my early years hanging around the old Madison Square Garden on Eighth Avenue at 49th Street. In those days, life at the Garden encompassed a wide variety of personalities involved in numerous sports and one of them was Angelo Dundee who was, of course, the trainer to a wild young talent out of Louisville, Kentucky called Cassius Clay. I first met Angelo back in 1963 and he soon had me helping him with his boxers whenever they needed treatment for muscle strains and joint pain.

In 1966, we were preparing the man now known as Muhammed Ali when he suffered a hamstring problem just a couple of days before his fight with Zora Folley. The injury had probably occurred while he was running in nearby Central Park in those heavy military style boots he used to wear to strengthen his legs.

Angelo had me treating the leg for an hour in the morning and an hour in the afternoon in those last days before the fight. Being the fit and beautifully honed athlete that he was, he responded to the ice packs and therapeutic ultrasound treatments I administered. I don't know whether he felt the hamstring pain during the fight but it hardly mattered. Foley didn't last long!

Strangely enough, my co-author, Richard Evans, and I discovered we were both working that fight. Richard was the New York correspondent for the London Evening News at the time. Richard remembers Clay sitting on the edge of the ring one afternoon when he had finished training and entertaining the New York press corps with a string of outrageous stories because he had been told the tickets weren't selling fast enough. Inevitably the headlines which followed the next day took care of that!

But with me, there was none of the boastful public bravado on which he built his reputation. The young man was polite and cooperative and always asked about my family. All that yelling and screaming for the cameras was just a pre-meditated and very successful attempt to make sure that his incredible talent did not go unrecognized.

By the time, I joined the tennis tour all that seemed like a different world which, indeed, it was. Boxing and tennis may be similar in that they demand one-on-one combat between two highly trained individuals but there the likeness ends. Boxing, inevitably, attracted its share of dubious individuals but Angelo gained a justified reputation as one of the best men in the sport and he was always great with me.

In tennis, I witnessed the full gamut of emotions. There were hilarious moments; times of extreme tension and high stress and inevitably some quarrels as huge egos clashed. I learned how to step away and not be seen to take sides because that would have been fatal. I had to treat McEnroe one moment and Connors the next. These were two guys who disliked each other so much they wouldn't even agree to stay in the same hotel at a Davis Cup tie when they were supposed to be on the same team!

Happily, I have the kind of personality that can deal with big egos in highly stressful situations. If some nasty words were thrown my way occasionally, they arrived with amazing infrequency and in any case, I just let them roll away like water off the proverbial duck's back. (We had a duck in the locker room once, but that's a story for later). Those that were rude usually came back a little later and apologized. They knew where their next treatment was coming from!

When players are over wrought, the only thing to do is to back off and give them their space. Even if they are hurt and need fairly prompt treatment, it is wise to wait because you are not going to get compliance in any event. At the top of the professional tennis world, one is dealing with a very special type of human being – an ego-driven competitor the likes of which the normal person rarely encounters. Although some have also been very good in Davis Cup, which requires thinking about teammates for a change, the type that reaches the very top in tennis is basically not a team player. He is a self-motivated individualist to his core and one thing you learn very quickly about this kind of person is that, when pushed, he pushes back – hard. So you give them space, let them cool off and then ask them politely if they would like some treatment. If you get nothing more than a nod or a grunt, you're winning.

Over the past forty years, I suppose I have had a close up view of every type of personality and the behavior patterns that go with them. Some have been heart-warming and others made your toes curl. One of the most emotional was the night at Flushing Meadows when Andre Agassi played his last match at the US Open, losing, inappropriately really, to the journeyman German, Benjamin Becker. He had not really been fit enough to play. A couple of matches earlier, he collapsed in the parking lot, semi-paralyzed by the hip and lower back problems he was going through. But no matter what Andre said about hating tennis in his autobiography, he wasn't about to give up. He owed his New York fans one last hurrah and he did his best. But when he walked into the locker room after giving his tearful farewell speech on court, he flung his arms around my neck and practically fell into my arms. We both knew what he had been through during his entire career. I had first met Andre when his father brought him to the courts at Caesar's Palace during the Alan King Classic at the age of four and persuaded Jimmy Connors to hit with him. Once he joined the tour I had tried to keep him as fit enough to play which, towards the end, had become practically impossible. But Andre knew I understood and that I cared and he doesn't forget his friends.

On the other side of the coin, you see players lose self control and let themselves down. Marat Safin was a great player and a great personality on tour, but the big Russian had no control over his temper. At Indian Wells, tournament director Charlie Pasarell had gone to great lengths and expense to build fabulous locker rooms at his new stadium with beautiful wood doors on each locker. After losing a match towards the end of his career, Safin stormed in and put his racket through the door of his locker and then ripped it off its hinges.

But then, like another generally warm and pleasant guy, Goran Ivanisevic, Safin was an uncontrolled racket smasher. Apparently they needed an outlet for their anger and frustration but it wasn't pretty to watch.

At home in Boca Raton, Florida, life is quieter now, though no less interesting. Sports medicine continues to evolve at an amazing rate with new equipment appearing on the market every day. Through the contacts I have built up over the years, I usually manage to keep ahead of the new trends and often have items in my treatment room before they hit the market.

This helps to keep my current clients happy because they are a slightly different group from Sampras and Federer. There are kids from the Rick Macci Academy, the Evert Academy and USTA Player Development Academy starting out on their professional careers or just a bunch of guys and gals who love this game of tennis and are desperate to keep playing. As the latter pass forty, the state of their bodies doesn't always match that desire so I do the best I can to keep them going. This book is designed to keep you amused with inside stories from the tour while explaining in detail, ways of preventing and dealing with injuries and physical problems that relate specifically to tennis players and indeed, anyone who wants to keep physically active later in life.

The science of sports medicine is evolving every day and I make sure that I keep abreast of it. In that way, I am able to help people lengthen their active participation in all manner of athletic endeavors with tennis players, of course, forming the bulk of my client base. The Florida sun helps, of course, and I hope this book will, too.

Pain, Set & Match

SECTION I:

The Memories

Pain, Set & Match

Chapter 1: World Team Tennis

"Bill Norris was one of the first people involved in sport therapy during the early days of professional tennis. He was a great help to me – and to the other women on Tour. I respect his expertise so much that I still call on him to treat my family – and our students at the Evert Tennis Academy."

— Chris Evert

"For so many years Billy performed his job with a lighthearted professionalism that always made the training room a fun place to visit. He treated every player the same and had an amazing knack for figuring out ways to keep us healthy. He was a special part of the tour and everyone loved being around Billy because of his infectious enthusiasm for life."

— Mike Bryan

World Team Tennis, the brain-child of Billie Jean King and her husband of the time, Larry King, proved to be my stepping stone into tennis from the worlds of baseball and basketball.

It was the early seventies and tennis was on the verge of the boom that had been created by the advent of Open Tennis; Lamar Hunt's World Championship Tennis tour and the television coverage it attracted. WCT, while ground breaking in the levels of professionalism it brought to what, previously, had been a largely amateur, all-white, country club sport, was still relatively traditional in how it presented the game – at least as far as the scoring system was concerned. While a pioneer in so many ways, Lamar was quite conservative in his approach to life and wanted the waves he caused in any sport he bought into to be measured.

Billie Jean was less worried by what people thought and was always trying to think out of the box. She came from a working class family in Long Beach, California. She wanted to take her sport to the masses and worked feverishly to come up with ideas for doing that. She had the perfect partner in Larry who was an ideas man to his finger tips and backed her all the way.

World Team Tennis was not quite like anything anyone had ever seen before which was just the way Billie Jean wanted it. One set matches with tie-breaks at 5-5; colored clothing, multi-colored courts divided into strips of various hues; spectators actively encouraged to holler and cheer during points; music blaring at changeovers, the whole thing done and dusted in three hours – all this was as far removed from Wimbledon as Mars. And with tennis being as popular as it was in the seventies, it took off.

The Los Angeles Strings were led by their owner Jerry Buss. He had been a professor at USC where Bob Lutz had starred. Lutz would go on to win numerous doubles titles, including Wimbledon, with Stan Smith. A born entrepreneur, Buss made a fortune in real estate with a company called Mariani-Buss and one of the perks of playing on his team was the nice apartments we were all provided with during our time with the Strings. Later, in 1979, Buss bought the whole Inglewood Forum package, which included the Lakers and Kings, from the Canadian Jack Kent Cooke. The famous basketball team is still in the family – Jeanie Buss, Jerry's daughter, now runs the Lakers. Her boyfriend, Phil Jackson, was the Lakers coach for several seasons.

I had come into tennis in 1973 through WTT when Ted Cohen asked me to work for his Florida Flamingos team over on my side of the country in Miami. US Davis Cupper Frank Froehling was the coach and Maria Bueno, the graceful and charming Wimbledon champion from Brazil, was the star. She didn't actually play that much because of her elbow problems. She was taking a lot of cortisone shots – something I have never liked and always tried to use only as a short term solution.

Cliff Drysdale was also on the team. He was nearing the end of his playing career and had already made a name for himself off court in his role as President of the newly-formed Association of Tennis Professionals, leading them through the emotionally-draining Wimbledon boycott of 1973. Cliff, of course, would go on to enjoy a 30-year career commentating for ESPN, and he was always very helpful to me – opening up contacts and helping to channel my own career.

I had not been with the Flamingos very long before Buss made me an offer to train the Strings and I moved out to LA. I had introductions from people like Drysdale and Bob Briner, who would take over from Jack Kramer as CEO of the ATP. I soon found myself working regular ATP events as well as for Jack at the old Los Angeles Tennis Club. There he ran the Pacific Southwest, – one of the world's premier tournaments in those days. I also worked for Barry Mackay up in San Francisco when Mackay was staging his ATP event at the cavernous Cow Palace, a venue better known for staging huge political conventions and rodeos (thus Cow Palace).

To start with, WTT was my main gig and we had a wonderful cast of characters at the Strings. Breaking with tradition in true Billie Jean style, Rosie Casals became one of the first women ever to coach men when she was appointed to that role by Buss – with just a little bit of support from her good friend Billie!

During that first season in 1975, Rosie had Bob Lutz; the Aussie Wimbledon doubles champions Ross Case and Geoff Masters and Betty Ann Grubb as her team. They responded pretty well to a female coach despite the uniqueness of the situation in those days. However, in 1976, Dennis Ralston, the former US No 1 and Davis Cup captain, joined as the new coach as Buss opened his checkbook to beef up the squad. The major signing was Ilie Nastase, a huge star and ticket seller at that time. He had beaten Arthur Ashe in the US Open final five years before. Nasty, a nickname that seemed fitting even though Ilie was basically a kind and lovable rogue. He had established himself as one of the bad boys of international sport since that triumph at Forest Hills. While most people found his antics funny, he drove some people nuts. Unfortunately, one of them was Mark Cox, a very proper English gent who had graduated from Cambridge University and joined the Strings as the No 2 singles player. Nasty got right under Mark's skin but somehow they managed to co-exist. Whenever things got tense there was always Vijay Amritraj, the tall and elegant Indian, whose soothing humor could defuse the tensest situation. No one was surprised when, later in life, Vijay ended up as a UNICEF ambassador.

Big as Nastase was, he was certainly no bigger attraction than Chris Evert who had won the first of her six US Open titles in 1975. She joined us in '78 at the height of her popularity. She was America's sporting darling despite an on-court demeanor that earned her the tag of Little Miss Ice Maiden. What a great camouflage that was! Chris always said that she dare not reveal her true personality on court for fear of losing concentration. She is not alone amongst top players in keeping themselves in check during the heat of battle. Chrissie was an extreme case because she was really a fun loving girl with a naughty and often hilarious sense of the ridiculous. After breaking up with Jimmy Connors in 1974, she had boyfriends galore including Burt Reynolds who showed up in the locker room one night to take her off night clubbing for the evening. Not soon after, John Lloyd, the handsome British Davis Cup star began dating her and of course, they eventually got married.

Despite being such a single minded competitor, Chris quickly embraced the team concept and everyone loved having her around. On a team, nothing beats a super star who can mix it with everyone, have fun and yet keep winning.

There was another member of the Strings team that you should know about – William Clyde Tulley (WCT) the Second. Willie was a duck, a very elegant white duck. His predecessor had been William Clyde Tulley who was given to me by

Norman Arey, the tour's assistant PR guy, during a WCT event in Memphis. Hence, his initials WCT. Eventually, he went off to live with someone who had a farm and William Clyde the Second was brought on board to become the Strings' mascot. He lived in the locker room or sat courtside during matches in his little cage and may have quacked now and again. Especially, after slurping up some of the Fosters we put in a clean ashtray for him. It would have been difficult to hear above the noise of the crowd. He probably had conversations with Nastase, too. If Ilie had been prepared to try and talk to Cyclops, the original one-eyed line-calling device introduced at Wimbledon, the crazy Romanian certainly wasn't beyond having a chat to a slightly drunk duck. Willie did like his beer!

Nastase might have sworn at him occasionally, too, because Nasty was always pushing the limits of acceptable behavior. He once tried to pull my pants down during an on court ceremony. "You want crazy? I give you crazy!" he would yell whenever anyone suggested he was going too far. It was never dull.

Generally, our mascot was a tension-reliever. It was difficult to get mad with that duck waddling around the locker room. Given the wham-bam scoring system where sets – and therefore matches – were over before you could blink an eye, everyone was pretty pumped once the action started. Willie was a great morale lifter. He used to travel with us on the road and often would share a room with me. I used to run the bath and drop Willie in it and he'd swim around all night getting rid of his hangover.

If Willie thought he was the star of the show, he had some pretty stiff competition, not just with the players on our team but with the movie stars who used to turn up to watch us. Kenny Rogers was a true fan, as was Farah Fawcett who was big friends with Vijay Amritraj and his younger brother Ashok, who also played for the Strings. Ashok, in fact, soon gave up tennis and went into the movie business himself and is now an established Hollywood producer. Ed 'Cookie' Byrnes was another regular supporter as was that giant singer Ed Ames of the Ames Brothers. The playwright Neil Simon also used to come as did most of the Van Patten family, especially Dick and his son Vinnie who would go on to become an ATP pro. Vinnie was a fine tennis player and a tremendous athlete. One year in Tokyo he beat John McEnroe on his way to winning the prestigious Seiko event.

The biggest change WTT provided for me was the chance to work with women athletes. It was something I had never done before and anatomically, it offered a crash course in understanding the female body. Luckily, we did not have too many serious injuries in those days. Most matches were played on a felt carpet with plenty of 'give' and the Team Tennis format ensured that matches did not last very long.

I found that women tended to suffer a little bit more in the knee area than the men. They seemed to be more prone to tendon and ligament problems, especially behind the knee. And there was also medial tibial stress syndrome which can create what people refer to as shin splints.

But Chrissie and the rest of the girls were buying into the relatively new idea of preventative exercises and stretching which I insisted on. The concept of having a full time athletic trainer working with them was definitely something they were unaccustomed to and I was only there because Buss had the funding to pay for the position which was something not many other teams enjoyed.

At the Forum I worked in a little central room that had doors leading to both the men's and women's locker rooms but at some locations there was only one changing room! So the girls went in and changed first and the boys followed. Often the players would wrap up and go back to the hotel to shower when we were on the road. Considering the star power we had on the team with the potential for clashing of egos, it all worked pretty well and everyone developed a sort of brother-sister relationship.

It was a different era back then. There was less pressure, less media coverage and everyone seemed ready to embrace each other as individuals than they do now. Top players of the day like John Newcombe were quite happy to play mixed doubles. While Margaret Court usually travelled with her husband Barry, a large man who seemed perfectly content to wander about all day with their first baby cradled in one arm. Frequently the free arm would be used to lift a pint of beer!

I spent four happy summers with the Strings, culminating with our championship winning effort in 1978. The next year, Evert's contract had run out and Buss downgraded his financial commitment. This had big repercussions across the league as he had a controlling interest in two other teams as well. After a short hiatus, Billie Jean's energy and commitment ensured that WTT would revive and continue. New entrepreneurs like Mark Ein in Washington DC have actually gone as far as to build a stadium by the Potomac for his highly successful Washington Kastles team.

Luckily, I was able to make a seamless shift to working for the ATP as their first full time athletic trainer and 'full time' just about described it. I signed up for 40 weeks on the road and the fact that I am still happily married says an awful lot for Sherie's patience and understanding.

Chapter 2: Davis Cup

In my 13 years on the ATP Tour, Bill was the go-to guy when you needed help of any kind. A friendly face to see when you had any physical (and mental) issues that needed healing as well as a confidant and friend to all players. Bill is one of the true legends of men's professional tennis and the best informed and most trusted insider of his time in the game. A player had officially arrived on tour when Bill knew his name. You were a nobody until "Norton" was looking after you."

— Jim Courier

"Going into Bill's room for treatment made me feel I'd arrived on the ATP tour. No one else welcomed me like he did. It wasn't just getting a tape job, it was being made to feel part of the world of Ilie Nastase and John McEnroe and all the other greats. As a young player I was nervous but Bill calmed me down, told me to keep going and then offered up suggestions of which concert to go to. He was different, that's for sure."

— Mats Wilander

My fourteen year career as athletic trainer to the United States Davis Cup team began with me having to stitch up the shorts of a large Venezuelan with a very big behind!

I trust it can be said that I went on to greater things in the service of my country. In those days, some of the teams we found ourselves competing against arrived hopelessly ill-equipped. At the Tucson Racquet Club in 1975, Venezuela certainly didn't have a trainer nor, indeed, a needle and thread. I always carried such items, having learned how useful they could be during my days with the Mets and the Knicks. When Humphrey Hose bent over and split his shorts right up the back, I offered to help because there were evidently no spare shorts of the required size lying around.

Hose, who actually came from the island of Curacao, and Jorge Andrew, who is now running the new $1.7 million Lexington County Tennis complex at Oak Grove, South Carolina, were Venezuela's singles players. With Jimmy Connors, Roscoe Tanner, and Dick Stockton on the team, we were able to get Tony Trabert's first tie as captain off to a winning start.

Trabert was my first captain to be followed by Arthur Ashe and Tom Gorman. All three were very different people and inevitably, made very different captains. As a multiple Grand Slam singles winner and veteran of the Jack Kramer pro tour in the fifties and sixties, Trabert commanded immediate respect. Tony was older than his predecessor, Dennis Ralston, with whom I was to work with during my WTT days.

It had been Lutz, the burly Californian, who had recommended me for the job after our time together with the Los Angeles Strings. Bob was a fixture on the team in the mid-seventies along with Roscoe Tanner, Erik Van Dillen, Dick Stockton, Stan Smith, Brian Gottfried, Harold Solomon, Arthur Ashe, Fred McNair, and less frequently, Connors and Vitas Gerulaitis. They made for an interesting bunch of personalities but Trabert stamped his own air of authority on the squad. He was the most organized captain we ever had, very thorough but personable and not afraid to delegate. I soaked up everything he said like a sponge and enjoyed the fact that he left it to me to get the guys up in the morning and organize training times.

Trabert had learned the role from his own mentor and former doubles partner, Billy Talbert, who, by that time, was already established as a popular tournament director of the US Open. Tony brought dignity and tradition to the job in an age when the players were receiving no money for the honor of representing their country. They did get free uniforms, though, which was a big deal in those days, especially when, for a time, they were designed by the celebrity couturier Oleg Cassini.

The other member of the US Davis Cup during this entire period was Dr. Omar Fareed who, apart from being a fine doctor, was one of the kindest, sweetest people I ever knew. Unlike most of the medical staff employed by the tennis world today, Omar was not an orthopaedic doctor. He had considerable experience, having worked all over the world – Tibet, Vietnam, Hong Kong and especially in Africa where he spent time with Dr. Albert Schweitzer at his jungle hospital in Lambarene in the Gabon. As a result he was an expert on tropical disease and made sure the players did not pick up anything nasty on their travels.

He was very fastidious about what we ate and even in Sweden, would go into the hotel kitchen to check on cleanliness and the way the food was prepared. We were even told not to eat the canapés at embassy cocktail parties. "You never know how long that mayonnaise has been sitting around,", he would say.

Some years later his son, Dr. George Fareed, who captained the tennis team at the University of California before continuing his education in Nice, France, would succeed his father as Davis Cup doctor. But, like father, like son, George would not be satisfied with the luxury jobs and now spends much of his time near the Mexican border looking after children from destitute homes.

When Omar's daughters married into the tennis fraternity (Shireen to Charlie Pasarell and Marcie to Frank Craighill, one of Donald's Dell's original partners) it gave the entire US Davis Cup team setup even more of a family feel and it was something I did my best to foster during the fourteen years I was the group's care giver.

I suppose you need to have my kind of temperament to look back and say I really enjoyed my lengthy time as trainer to the US Davis Cup team. Of course, there were the great times when we won the trophy under Trabert in 1978 and '79 and with Ashe as captain in 1981 and '82. There were some stressful times, too!

Given the era, that was hardly surprising. Amateur officiating had not yet caught up with the behavior umpires and referees were being asked to handle. The game had never witnessed personalities like Jimmy Connors, John McEnroe, Vitas Gerulaitis, and Peter Fleming not to mention foreign stars like that volatile Romanian Ilie Nastase.

Even Trabert and Ashe struggled to control them at times and there were moments when the umpires simply lost the plot. And of course, trips to Latin America, where the partisan crowds had no interest in anything other than stirring up the atmosphere to boiling pitch, just rubbed raw nerves to the bone.

However, no matter what people have said about McEnroe, he never shied away from what he considered a duty to represent his country. Even when a visit to Argentina was on the agenda – where the presence of those world-class clay court experts Guillermo Vilas and Jose-Luis Clerc made our chances almost impossible – John showed up and did his best. He always stepped up to play.

Trouble did not only erupt abroad. A tie in Portland, Oregon against Australia seemed to bring out the worst in everyone with McEnroe's outbursts. This was fully supported by the not-always-angelic Fleming. It tested Ashe's diplomacy to its limits. McEnroe didn't think Arthur was giving him enough support in John's dispute with the chair umpire over line calls while Ashe, McEnroe's polar opposite in temperament, was trying not to show just how appalled he was at some of the things being said by McEnroe.

But there were plenty of great moments, too, like the Davis Cup epic in St Louis when McEnroe and Mats Wilander battled for 6 hours 22 minutes to create a record for longevity in Davis Cup tennis history. It was the sort of match no one deserved to lose but McEnroe etched himself into the annals of the competition as one of the great Davis Cup fighters by winning 9-7, 6-2, 15-17, 3-6, 8-6. The score tells some of the story – the grueling third set and the need for John to remain un-phased and totally determined in the face of the Swede's comeback.

They were both young, of course, but even so the way they were both moving in the last hour or so was amazing. Wilander covered acres of court across his baseline as McEnroe darted in to angle his volleys and the crowd was frequently left gasping at the skill and athleticism of this remarkable pair of athletes. No, they didn't hit the ball as hard as the likes of Rafa Nadal and Novak Djokovic – wood rackets were being used, remember – but the skill on display was no less inferior for that.

I had done my best to keep John hydrated throughout with electrolyte drinks – mostly Gatorade. His ability to battle on for such an incredible length of time was remarkable considering how little hard training he put in off the court. That did not impair his ability to move like lightening around the court. Adrenaline kicks in, of course, in the heat of battle and as much as anything, that's what kept him going.

Nevertheless it was remarkable that neither player suffered from cramps during the physical ordeal, even allowing for the fact that the tie was played indoors. More remarkable, I suppose is the fact that never, during my entire time with the US Davis Cup team, did I have a player go down with cramps other than Jimmy Arias in a dead rubber in Sweden. I firmly believe that was due to the tension that existed within the squad during that unhappy encounter in 1984. Pete Sampras, of course, pushed himself past his limit against Russia at the Olympic Stadium in Moscow and had to be half carried and half dragged off court but I was no longer working with the team by then.

If I have to pin point one reason why this was so, I suppose I would settle on the little electrolyte tablets I handed out to the players before every match. They were the same tablets I got from Champion Nutrition labs in Texas, which as you can read in the Nandrolone chapter, became so controversial some years later when players started testing positive for steroids. There was nothing illegal about the tablets but, until Richard

Ings, the ATP Tour rules administrator, proved otherwise, a batch was suspected of being contaminated with steroid drugs.

Along with Gatorade, which serves the same function, the tablets worked for our players in Davis Cup and even on the tour, there were comparatively few instances of players cramping during my tenure with the ATP. Even Michael Chang, who was suffering from cramps when, at the age of 17, he upset Ivan Lendl at the French Open, never suffered from cramps again.

By the time Tom Gorman took over the captaincy from Ashe in 1986 everything was marginally more relaxed. Tom certainly had the right personality for the job with his ready smile and reputation as a straight shooter. He had set his own standards of sporting behavior at the year-end Masters finals in Barcelona in 1972 when he reached match point against Stan Smith in the semi-final and then walked stiffly up to the net to shake hands and concede the match. Gor's back had 'gone' a few points earlier and knowing the extent of the chronic condition as he did, he realized he would be in no shape to play the final. So, rather than risk depriving the tournament of its showpiece, he quit. There have been few more honorable reasons for doing so.

Gorman was well organized, too, and ran a good ship although he did fret over how to handle McEnroe's unpredictable moods from time to time! During a long eight year reign as captain, Gorman ushered in the new generation of American stars and we had Andre Agassi, Jim Courier and Jay Berger on the squad in Peru, along with those two stalwarts, Arias and Aaron Krickstein when the US defeated Pablo Arraya and his colleagues in Lima. Unfortunately that turned out to be my last tie. Political storms were blowing through the game again and I became a victim.

Raymond Moore and Harold Solomon, brought in Hamilton Jordan as the ATP CEO. Jordan had been the Chief of Staff for President Jimmy Carter. The famous parking lot press conference at Flushing Meadows followed when Jordan announced the breakaway from the Pro Council and the formation of a new ATP Tour. This was to be a fifty-fifty partnership with the tournament directors. Inevitably, the revolution caused a lot of animosity and Jordan did not want any ATP employee to have anything to do with the ITF which, of course, ran the Davis Cup.

I had always done my best to skirt around the game's politics and concentrate on my job of looking after tennis players. Jordan, who was not a tennis person but very much a politician, was adamant and to my disappointment, he did not get any argument from two of his senior lieutenants, Ron Bookman and Jim McManus. Both were colleagues of mine and I had hoped that they would plead my case but it did not turn out that way. Obviously, the ATP was my primary job (the Davis Cup never took up more than four weeks a year) so I had no choice but to accept Jordan's decision. Jordan, having achieved what he had been brought in to do, did not stay long and Mark Miles soon arrived from Indianapolis to begin his long tenure as ATP boss.

Miles, a pragmatic leader and skilled negotiator, did not lay down such hard and fast rules about what his employees could do but by that time the Davis Cup job had been filled and I never got it back.

I did, however, spend two happy years with the Indian Davis Cup team. That was in 1998, ten years after I had stopped working for the United States squad. Jaidip Mukerjea, who I had looked after when he was a player on the tour, was captain and of course, I knew members of his squad such as Mahesh Bhupathi and Leander Paes who were just starting their long careers which, amazingly, continue to this day! After I was approached, I had a conference call with R.K.Khanna, the authoritarian President of the Indian Tennis Association and agreed to terms.

They turned out to be a fun group to work with but we had to get our priorities straight and one of the first orders of business on arriving in Nottingham for the first tie of my tenure against Great Britain was to find a suitable Indian restaurant. In England that's never a problem and there was one very close to the Holiday Inn near east Midlands Airport where we were staying. The British team was installed in some splendor at the Breadsall Priory in Derby, a converted mansion house, but we had our budget limitations! I have always tried to advise players about their diets but it is no use trying to interfere with Indians and their curry. Nor was there any need to – it is what they like, what their systems are used to and they play well on it. That's all that matters!

Despite Bhupathi and Paes winning the doubles, Greg Rusedski and Tim Henman had taken care of the singles on the opening day and when Tim beat Leander in the fourth rubber it was all over.

The following year we were drawn to play South Korea in the Asian Zone. It made a nice change for me after years of travelling south of the border in the Americas. The weather did not cooperate and we found ourselves freezing in Sogwipo City on Cheju Island. So much so that we wore parkas at courtside and not enjoying the cold, my Indian colleagues went down 3-2 to Hyung-Taik Lee and Dong-Hyun Kim.

Happily, our next tie was at home in Calcutta at the South Club against China and we won that one 5-0. At the dinner I was presented with a smart Indian jacket and trousers but sadly it turned out to be a parting present. According to Khanna, the association could no longer afford me and a very enjoyable passage in my career came to an early end.

Chapter 3: The Grand Slams

"When I first hit the tour as an eighteen year old, not everyone was happy to see a new face around the locker room. It was tough to make friends but Bill made me feel at home right away. Despite the age difference, he was my first real friend on the tour and I'll always be grateful for the way he helped me through the early years."

— Andy Roddick

"Bill was a multitasker – joking with Scotty Davis over in that corner; offering a piece of quick advice to a guy just going on court; telling someone else he'd be right there with the massage and all the while doing the fastest, most expert tape job on my ankle, barely looking at it. We all went to Bill in a crisis – not because the other athletic trainers weren't good but because Bill had the experience, knew what he was talking about and perhaps most important of all, he made you feel good."

– Pat Cash

Slams are all different and I loved them all – for their variety and for the different challenges they offered.

If I say that Wimbledon is my favorite because of its tradition and the style with which they do things at the All England Club that is not to say that it offered the easiest working conditions, especially in the beginning. I had to overcome aspects of that tradition as far as becoming accepted as part of the scene during The Championships. Back in the seventies, there was so much resistance to the ATP's medical presence at the Championships that I was not allowed to treat players on the club grounds at all! The All England Club felt they would dictate who would treat all of the players in the Championships. The club wanted their own physiotherapists even if I did take care of the ATP players the rest of the year! I worked in a house the ATP was renting opposite the club on

Bathgate Road which was not terribly convenient for players who needed to come and see me.

But, happily, I got on with John Matthews, the official AELTC physiotherapist, right from the start and we used to communicate with each other by phone over the condition of various players in our care. I first met John when WCT held a tournament in London's Earl's Court in 1977. After that week we soon became friends. A willingness to compare notes and talk through whatever treatment was needed was to everyone's benefit.

Eventually, when Butch Buchholz was head of the ATP, I was allowed to move across the street and actually work on site. With his charm and ability to assuage people's fears, Butch had made the Wimbledon committee realize that it would be far better for the players to have someone they knew from the tour working alongside their own man.

I don't think you could call our working conditions spacious. The old No 1 locker room was considered first class back in the early eighties but the medical staff did not have a lot of space. There was another area downstairs where we were able to install some equipment like a deep heat machine and create a little workout room with a Versa-climber. But, in those days, it was all quite rudimentary.

Richard Greer, a soft-spoken and very English gentleman, was the No 2 to the club secretary (Chris Gorringe during most of my years working there) and I believe, still carries out that role today. Once he accepted the growing aspects of professionalism that were creeping into the game, he was very amenable to our demands and helped me a good deal. Meanwhile, inside the locker room, there was a pint-sized cockney character called Leo Turner who ran the place with a cheerful smile on his face. Older readers who used to watch Wimbledon in those days may remember him as the little chap in a white coat who carried the players' rackets onto Centre Court on finals day.

There are no white coats at the US Open. New York provides a very different atmosphere and always did, even in the more genteel surroundings of the West Side Tennis Club at Forest Hills where the championships were held before the move to Flushing Meadows in 1978.

My association with the event actually came about when the Westside Tennis Club hired me to work at Forest Hills. Those familiar with the property will know that the main stadium is situated quite a long walk from the old clubhouse which is where I found myself working – in a small room on the third floor! There was a massage therapist working in the bowels of the stadium but any player with an injury had to climb those stairs to reach me. If he took the trouble, you knew he was really in need of help!

The decision of USTA, with President Slew Hester, was to move the event to Flushing Meadows. This move was huge for the game. The Louis Armstrong stadium allowed for larger crowds. The locker rooms in those early days were housed across the walkway in the old indoor tennis center. The training room was upstairs from the indoor courts. Up there I had a little bit more space to work. In fact, I needed it because the start of the US Open was always one of the busiest times of the year for me as players desperately tried to shake off the effects of the summer season on those unforgiving North American hard courts.

We did our best to patch them up but there were always early round defaults as there continue to be today. A tournament can handle defaults in the first or second rounds because they get lost in the mass of activity taking place on all the outside courts and the referee has the option of moving matches into the main stadium should injuries occur there.

However, it is a totally different deal on finals day and in 1983, we were facing a full blown crisis when Jimmy Connors hobbled in with a little toe he had injured by bashing his foot with that steel T-2000 racket of his while Ivan Lendl got hit with an attack of diarrhea. Only one of them needed to be unfit and you didn't have a final! Suddenly there was an aura of panic about the place.

Lendl had lost to Connors in the 1982 final and was still searching for his first Grand Slam title. With stomach problems, it is often difficult to pin point the cause and I was never sure whether Ivan had eaten something tainted or was just suffering from nerves. Either way one tablet of Imodium seemed to do the trick but Connors was a different story.

Donald Dell, whose company ProServ was looking after both finalists, has said recently that he found a physician from the Jets at nearby Shea Stadium to come over and give Connors an injection in his little right toe. I have no recollection of that. As far as I am concerned, Jimmy's situation was handled entirely by Doctor Irving Glick, the US Open's much loved and long serving medical officer. We both knew that the injection which the good doctor gave Jimmy before the match would only last for about 90 minutes and then a decision would have to be made.

In those days, you were only allowed to leave the court for a bathroom break. But this was the final of the US Open with a packed stadium and CBS beaming the match live across America and to the rest of the World. By his own account, Dell had spoken to Billy Talbert, the tournament director, and I assume they came to some understanding of what was required in the greater scheme of things.

At any rate, after a couple of sets, it became clear that there was no way Connors was going to be able to continue without another injection. Doctor Glick realized what a default would mean and very reluctantly, agreed to administer a second injection of Novocain in the little room underneath the stand that links Armstrong stadium to the adjacent Grandstand Court.

The room is really a toilet, just to the left as you walk off Armstrong, big enough for wheelchair access with a toilet and a sink. I remember very clearly ushering Jimmy in there and

Doctor Glick and I were the only other people present when the injection was administered.

It worked and Connors went on to win his sixth US Open title 6-0 in the fourth after Lendl had won the second set.

The thing to remember here is that both players were suffering and we had done our best for both of them. Neither would have wanted to give up or win by default. They were simply too competitive for that. Connors, of course will always be remembered as a player that never gave up. He was prepared to spill his blood on court in search of victory. Lendl was not much different which may have contributed to the fact that they really didn't like each other! Ivan often played with illnesses and injuries that would have stopped most players from competing; ignoring the best medical advice we had to offer. There was no way that these two highly driven personalities wanted to beg off and not play. When you have two athletes that are so committed they will always go against medical advice. They both were determined to give the spectators a great finals match. That is professionalism at its best.

I laugh when I hear people say the French are difficult to deal with. Right from the word go I found the French Open the most cooperative and friendly of the Slams. Philippe Chatrier, who went on to be a much-admired President of the ITF, was the architect of the modernized Roland Garros, of course, and he set the tone. Patrice Clerc and Christian Duxin, who took over as Chatrier faded from the scene – unhappily a victim of Alzheimer's – were always charming to me and I quickly became great friends with their chief physio, Robert Laurens, who has retired now but is still a regular visitor during the championships.

A great deal of rebuilding went on during the years I worked there with entire stands being knocked down and rebuilt within the required 50 week time frame. In some ways Chatrier was a dreamy visionary but he knew how to crack the whip and get things done. As a result our working conditions in the spacious new locker rooms improved beyond recognition and of course, the medical staff were first class. Dr. Bernard Montalvant and Dr. Jean-Pierre Cousteau, a relative of the famous under-water explorer Jacques Cousteau, were always ready to give the players their best advice. I have always had that feeling when dealing with the medical profession in France. Walk into any Pharmacie in any town and you invariably find yourself facing someone behind the counter who is not only concerned and helpful but really seems to know what they are talking about. One invariably gets the best up to date medicines in France.

The only 'contretemps', as the French would call it, that I had to deal with at Roland Garros came about because of a little jealous rivalry between the tournament's medical staff and the people who ran the First Aid center for the public. As you would expect, the public infirmary was very well run by properly-qualified personnel but, understandably perhaps, they felt a little left out of the action which, at a big tennis tournament, is always in the locker rooms. They wanted in but Robert and the doctors were not at all keen on the idea. I had come to know both groups well over the years and wearing my best diplomatic hat, I persuaded the infirmary guys that it was just not going to happen and eventually they accepted the fact with a modicum of good grace.

The US Open and Australian Open have changed most noticeably over the years, primarily, of course because they both left their traditional homes at Forest Hills and Kooyong, quitting the confines of a private club for the modern expanse of public facilities at Flushing Meadows and Melbourne Park.

But it is the Australian that has changed the most because, during those last years at Kooyong, it was struggling to maintain its Grand Slam status with low prize money and poor entries. Had not Brian Tobin, the President of what would become known as Tennis Australia, been far-sighted enough to persuade the Victoria State Premier, John Cain, to fund the development at what was originally called Flinders Park, it is highly likely Australia could have lost its Grand Slam to a city in Asia.

But, no matter what political dramas were swirling around, I think we all enjoyed the last years at Kooyong. Inevitably, the clubhouse bar was a focal point of activity as the sun went down every evening but one evening the men's locker room enjoyed a bit of entertainment, too. Led by Chris Evert and Pam Shriver, a group of women players decided to pay the boys a visit! I remember the looks on some of the guy's faces as a bunch of giggling girls walked in. To their disappointment (I think) no one was walking around totally nude just at that moment but the college-style prank was enjoyed by all and after Chrissie (so different behind the scenes compared with her focused demeanor on court) called out, "Just wanted to find out what you guys were up to in here!" everyone had a good laugh and settled down for some light hearted chat.

The move to the brand new complex by the River Yarra, a mere ten minute walk from downtown Melbourne, lifted the championships into a different world and Ted Tinling, the great couturier and PR officer for the WTA Tour, was right on the button as usual when he announced on the 15,000 seat Centre Court with its sliding roof, "Ladies and Gentlemen, you are looking at the future!"

Perhaps even Ted, who, even in his late seventies, was always abreast of the next happening, could not have envisaged how quickly the Australian Open, originally under the direction of Colin Stubs and then Paul McNamee, would embrace the future, adding a second stadium with a roof and expanding across the railway yards to create one of the game's great venues.

With much more space and everyone offering such a warm Aussie welcome, it was a pleasure to work there. But, of course, there were some teething problems and one day, in the middle of a mighty storm, it became apparent that greater defenses were needed against the River Yarra which burst its banks and turned the stadium into a swimming pool. I remember seeing some of the ground staff swim across it!

There was another incident in Melbourne that showed how accidents can happen in the most unlikely fashion. Cyril Suk, the top Czech doubles player, whose sister Helena Sukova, was a Wimbledon singles finalist, was walking past a huge hot water urn on his way into the unseeded players' locker room. The strap on his tennis bag got hooked onto the faucet and pulled the whole thing over, splashing scalding water all over Suk's foot and lower leg. Poor Cyril was in agony as the tournament physician, Dr. John Fraser, brother the 1960 Wimbledon champion Neale, treated him and got him off to the hospital. The burns were so bad they kept him in the hospital for a week.

Happily, that was a once off incident and my memories of Australia are of sunny skies and sunny people who, even under the extra pressure that a Grand Slam brings, always managed to appear laid back and positive. Maybe it's because that so many of us were arriving from Northern Hemisphere winters that made the Australian Open so particularly appealing. I understand the International Tennis Writer's Association keep voting it the most friendly of the Grand Slams. I can well understand why.

Chapter 4: The ATP, Nandrolone and Me

In a career spanning more than forty years I have been incredibly lucky to have avoided major controversies and nasty arguments. I like to think that, apart from luck, my temperament has had something to do with that. I am not, by nature, a confrontational person. I am quite the opposite in fact.

There was one moment in my career when a great wave of turbulence hit pro tennis right where I lived – right in my training room. In 2003, routine drug tests carried out by Steffan Sahlstrom from Stockholm, who headed the ATP drug testing program, suddenly started showing over forty players failing to meet the two nanogram limit when tested for the anabolic steroid nandrolone.

This knocked us sideways. Right out of nowhere a significant number of players who had been competing in different parts of the world, as far apart as Europe and South America, were showing up positive. I was dumbfounded and so were all my ATP colleagues.

Richard Ings, the former umpire who was our executive vice president of rules and competition, began a top-to-bottom investigation as to the possible causes of this and unhappily for me, everything pointed to the jars of electrolyte tablets that all the athletic trainers dispensed at tournaments.

As the senior sports medicine athletic trainer I was not only in charge of this but I was the actual provider of the tablets. And the most perplexing thing was that I had been doing it for thirty years. And not just that – the tablets had been coming from exactly the same source for thirty years – a company called Champion Nutrition that was based in Arlington, Texas just outside Dallas. It was little more than a Mom & Pop outfit run by a woman named Kaye Droke and her husband. They had no more than three or four employees and were as legitimate as could be. I had become good friends with Kaye and had visited her lab on numerous occasions. To the best of my knowledge, they manufactured nothing more sinister than vitamin pills and electrolytes which seemed to rule out the only viable suggestion that had been put forward as an explanation – namely, that some nandrolone particles had been left on a work bench and been inadvertently swept into the make up of our electrolytes. The truth is that Champion Nutrition never made products that contained nandrolone or any other steroids.

This was the most frequently presented explanation when the media cross-questioned ATP officials because it seemed to be the only possible answer. The ATP lawyer Mark Young took a jar of the tablets and had 500 of them tested. They were all clean. This led Mark to tell the press: "We have been unable to prove that the electrolyte tablets were contaminated but they were the only common denominator in these cases."

That much was thought to be true at the time but it did not provide an answer.

Before I continue with this sad tale and bring in Greg Rusedski, let me explain a little about nandrolone. It is a member of the anabolic steroid family and helps promote stamina and recovery from strong physical exertion. That has been sufficient for some athletes to risk the rather alarming number of side effects such as the expansion of cardiac muscles which can help induce hearts attacks; promote the growth of facial bones and teeth; induce breast growth in men and facial hair in women as well as baldness and male impotence. Quite a list and one from which any sane person would run a mile but, of course, the intensity of modern competition at the highest levels of international sport encourages athletes to do some really stupid things.

Sadly, there have been plenty of them, assuming, of course, that they were all guilty. Those found to be guilty include the Olympic sprinters Linford Christie and Marlene Ottey; international soccer players like Christophe Dugarry of France and Edgar Davids of Holland; the Pakistan cricketer Shoaib Akhtar, who was exonerated after three months, as well as our own Petr Korda, the former Australian Open champion who was tested positive at Wimbledon after playing Tim Henman in 1998 and was banned for a year. Korda never played again.

The amount of nandrolone found in these players bodies varied a great deal. And this is where the whole problem becomes very unclear. Even though some of the track and field stars were found to have higher levels, all the tennis players were found to be only fractionally above the permitted amount that WADA and the IOC doping authorities allowed. And you want to know how miniscule that is? Two nanograms which, spelled out, looks like this: 0.000 000 002. Rusedski, for instance, tested at 0.000 000 005. That amount wouldn't help a bed bug hop onto a sheet.

Two nanograms was the limit set by the doping authorities who were going by the best research they had to work with at the time although one has to question whether it was 'best'. In determining what level to set for a positive or negative nandrolone test, the International Olympic Committee carried out tests at the WINTER Olympics. As Ings was to discover after his rather more rigorous investigation, they would have come up with different results had they tested athletes competing in tropical heat.

This is all part of the problem. There is no end to medical research. It is constantly evolving. What is gospel today may not be gospel tomorrow. As things change, the athlete can become a victim.

In the late nineties, a medical paper was published stating categorically that nandrolone could not be produced naturally in the human body. Oops! A few years later it was discovered that it can. Pregnant women produce significant amounts of the stuff. Then researchers at the University of Aberdeen in Scotland came up with findings that suggested anyone eating a big steak after strenuous exercise could produce more than two nanograms. At first this finding was discredited but as more evidence was produced, it is now more readily accepted provided the animals in question have been injected with steroids – a practice that is illegal in most countries but which can occur.

But respected experts like Professor Arne Ljundqvist had gone on record as saying, "People have tried to make nandrolone mysterious but it is the oldest known steroid. To test positive, you have to take something."

Like steak? I don't think that's what he meant.

Before the Rusedski affair hit the headlines, the only player out of the batch testing positive to be named was the Czech Bohdan Ulihrac because he was one of the first cases and was found guilty before the full extent of the problem became known. As soon as it became apparent that a large percentage of the tour was involved, his suspension was terminated. He was allowed to go straight back on the circuit. By then, however, his ranking had slipped and he had to qualify. Lacking match practice, he lost in the first round. Life isn't fair.

The last person to be tested over the limit was Rusedski, the British Davis Cup player and 1997 US Open finalist. By the time the tour went Down Under at the beginning of 2004, rumors were rife in the player lounges on the tour that Greg had been tested positive. Some people were saying it was for the designer steroid THG. But the rumors didn't last long because in an extraordinary move that some thought courageous and others foolhardy, Rusedski broke cover just before the Australian Open and announced that he had, indeed, been tested positive, but for nandrolone, not THG. The test had taken place at Indianapolis in the summer, some three months after the initial panic had seen the tour withdraw all pills, tablets, vitamins, electrolytes or supplements from the locker rooms.

Rusedski's move was surprising because he didn't have to do it. The ATP has always been very careful not to reveal anyone's name until the player is found guilty. As a result Ulihrac and Rusedski are the only two players from the 45 who tested positive during that time frame whose names are known. Once the ATP CEO, Mark Miles, and Richard Ings had reluctantly come to the conclusion that my tablets provided the only conceivable explanation, they admitted that the ATP had shown lack of care in administering supposedly contaminated pills to the players, this eliminated all sanctions. All those who had kept quiet were to remain anonymous forever.

That led to a stream of headlines in the media about ATP incompetence, etc. and inevitably, Miles took some stick. Checking back on the website now, my name seems curiously absent. Either some reporters were being kind or they didn't dig hard enough because I was an undeniable link in the chain if one believed the contaminated tablet theory.

So much so, that I was asked to testify before the three person tribunal in Montreal that was convened to sit in judgment on Rusedski on March 9th, 2004. The location was ironic because Montreal was Greg's birthplace and it was obviously not the reason he would have wanted to return to his parent's hometown. Nor did he enjoy my testimony. All I did was relate the facts as I have laid out here. The tablets had come from the same lab in Texas that they had always come from. I had no reason to believe Kaye Droke's business practices had changed in the thirty years I had been dealing with her. Champion Nutrition has never made products that contained Nandrolone or any products that contained steroids.

There was also a question about the length of time between the ATP banning all supplements from the locker rooms in early spring and Rusedski testing positive in Indianapolis three months later. I testified that the tablets turned black and smelly after a certain amount of time when released from a sealed jar and that it was unlikely that anyone would want to ingest them. But, on the other side of the coin, there was no hard and fast evidence as to how long traces of nandrolone stay in the body so the tribunal could find no reason to disassociate Rusedski's case from those of all the other players who had tested positive. And on that basis, he was cleared.

Unhappily, it took a little longer to repair our relationship. Greg obviously objected to the fact that I was testifying and if the looks he threw at me across the room during the proceedings could have killed, I would have been in trouble! It was not a position I enjoyed being in because my loyalty has always been to the players but, as an ATP employee, I really had no option but to do what I was asked. I think most players, like Andy Roddick and Andre Agassi who spoke out on my behalf, believed that I was an honest person and would tell the truth. Of course, that is what I did.

Anyway, Greg and I are on speaking terms again and he has gone on to carve out a new career for himself in British tennis by taking charge of the Junior Davis Cup team that triumphed in Mexico in 2011.

The only victim of this affair appeared to be Paul Settles, a popular ATP road manager and former college player of high standard. Paul had moved into a position whereby he was signing off on the checks I used to buy the electrolyte tablets. I have no idea as to the official reason for his leaving the ATP. But the fact is he resigned shortly after this whole affair blew up. He took a college tennis coaching job and has had a successful career.

As I have said, I had no logical explanation as to why so many players were suddenly testing positive and why the problem did not continue. If one batch of tablets was contaminated, I had no idea how or why. But it certainly changed the way we went about things on the tour. It was not only supplements that were banned from the locker rooms. Caffeine drinks were put on the 'verboten' list. Some tournaments went as far as limiting the amount of coffee that was allowed. Those pods you can put in some machines were tested for caffeine levels. Electrolyte drinks came under suspicion and could only be dispensed in sealed bottles rather than the huge vats we used to prepare. The word 'paranoia' was not far from people's minds and players became wary or even downright scared to take anything – even an aspirin.

This, of course, was not what we wanted to see because painkillers are an essential part of an athlete's life but some players opted for the pain rather than risk banishment.

Eventually, thanks to Ings' relentless determination to come up with an explanation, all the fear was proved to be unfounded. Richard, or Skippy, as he was called during his days as a young umpire (Australian – kangaroo – skip, if you follow the logic) decided to employ a high tech lab in Cologne, Germany to analyze buckets of urine that had been taken from the players after playing in a variety of conditions. As a result of their work, a way to determine whether a sample derived from synthetic or natural sources was discovered. In other words they could tell if you had ingested it or just produced it naturally in your own body.

Richard, who now runs his own company in Canberra, was kind enough to bring us up to date on what he had finally determined. "Following the withdrawal of all electrolyte tablets from the locker rooms, all incidences of low level nandrolone readings stopped," he explained.

"However, some month's later more low level readings appeared and continued to appear for over a year. This contributed to our eventual conclusion that the electrolyte tablets supplied to the tour were not the common cause of the rash of low level nandrolone readings and that they were, in fact, the result of nandrolone production in the body."

This was the final vindication for me and dear Kaye Droke who has now passed. This vindication was good to hear. What Ings did add was that IRMS tests had shown a common link with athletes who had engaged in long, heavy exercise routines in extremely hot climates. This suggested that by setting the limit at two nanograms after testing solely in a cold climate, the IOC had missed out on a significant factor in determining whether the readings came from natural nandrolone production in the body or as a result of having taken the drug synthetically. When one is dealing with a matter that can besmirch an athlete's reputation and ruin a career, I think the authorities have a duty to be a little more thorough. Ings certainly was and athletes in every sport, let alone those ATP players who fell under suspicion, owe him and that lab in Cologne a debt of gratitude.

We had gone from supplying useful electrolytes that were perfectly legal to worrying about every single thing a player put into his body for reasons that originated from fear and ignorance. In the end the whole exercise turned out to be worthwhile but, almost inevitably, the pendulum had swung too far, as it so often does in all walks of life. Who would have thought a virtual total ban on smoking would have come into effect so quickly? Some of us are old enough to remember the day when the majority of seats on an aircraft were designated as smoking areas with the non-smokers stuck in a little section at the back. How times change.

The same could be said for the social substances that players used to consume on tour. No one was thinking about steroids in the days of Rod Laver, Roy Emerson and John Newcombe – just how many beers they could get down and still function the next day. Players of today simply don't believe the stories you tell them about Emmo having fourteen beers the night before playing a best of five set final against Fred Stolle. But I can assure it happened. It was mostly beer which is relatively easy to run out of your system if you are young and fit, and Newk was not averse to the occasional Flaming Tequila at the end of a good party. Sometimes they singed his moustache.

The drinking culture amongst the Aussies was such that, on the WCT tour, they created a rule, which insisted everyone had to be in the bar for the first beer of the evening by 7.00 pm or face a fine. Those were the happy days at outdoor tournaments where there was no evening play. It didn't last long, of course, but Emmo and his drinking pals like Ray Ruffels, Bob Carmichael, Dick Crealy and Colin Dibley still found plenty of time to get stuck into 'the sauce' as they would call it.

Social drugs were not on the scene back in those days of the sixties and early seventies but it did not take long for that to change. Marijuana was emerging back then and cocaine became available at practically every party the smart set would go to. And the tennis stars were always welcome. It was the days of Studio 54 in New York and other fashionable night spots like Les Jardins in Dallas and I got the impression that too many very rich hangers-on were handing out too much 'stuff'. But no matter what had gone on the night before I never had one instance of a player appearing in my room in an unfit state to play.

The first drug testing on the ATP tour began in 1982 when Butch Buchholz was CEO and the idea was voted in by the players themselves. Tennis should be proud of the fact that it was the first sport to have players voluntarily vote in testing even though it could not have been terribly efficient right at the beginning.

The issue of drugs in sport will not go away and only education will help reduce their use. Steroids are incredibly harmful and athletes who take them are likely to pay a huge price later in life. But the testing must be thorough and follow research that is up to date at all times. No one deserves to be found guilty because someone didn't apply the correct criteria.

Chapter 5: Coaches

"I can't think of how many times in my pro career that Bill saved me during the week. Never short on ease and grace, he'd come out during an injury time out and greet me with a warm smile. Even when I knew I was hurting, something about the way he'd say, you're gonna be fine, immediately I'd believe him. He's got the gift, the knowledge, the trust and camaraderie of all the players he's ever worked with, in this business, Bill is a rare breed."

— Brad Gilbert

"Bill Norris has been a fixture in men's tennis for over 35 years. His knowledge and expertise in Sports Medicine as an athletic trainer has helped sustain and resurrect many top international players careers. I have had the pleasure to know him professionally and personally since 1979 through both my playing and coaching career. He has been invaluable on countless occasions and I would trust his opinion on Sports related injuries and recovery programs on many occasions. The Assoc. of Tennis Professionals was lucky to have a person as dedicated to his profession as Bill Norris. Thank you Billy for everything you have done for men's tennis!!"

— Larry Stefanki

It used to be simpler in the old days. There was Lennart Bergelin and there was me. Bergelin, the great gruff, genial Swede, was Bjorn Borg's coach. No one else had one. Certainly, no one had a coach that traveled the circuit.

Players like Rod Laver, John Newcombe or Roger Taylor used to come to me with all their aches and pains and accept my advice as to what treatment to receive and more critically, whether they were fit enough to play, because they had no one else to turn to.

As the money started pouring into the game in the seventies, more and more players took a look at how Bjorn was prospering with his father figure Lennart and began putting aside some of the money they were earning to hire a coach. Happily, I was well established on the tour by then and most of the newcomers understood that I was in charge of my treatment room and they consulted with me on injury problems. I made it my business to get on with the coaches no matter where they sprang from or what language they spoke because it was in the players' best interests, let alone mine, that we offered the best advice.

Bergelin obviously did a great job with Borg as a coach and father figure to the young Swede but there were occasions when I wondered whether Lennart's somewhat heavy handed massage technique was not doing more harm than good. Lennart was a big, gruff, jovial guy and he went at every aspect of his life with gusto. He certainly pummeled Bjorn's muscles and sometimes I was amazed he was able to walk the next day. I asked him about it on occasion but Bjorn just gave me one of his quiet little smiles and said, "Oh, it's ok, it dosen't hurt too much!"

Borg was one of the finest athletes we saw on the tour and he rarely got hurt. The one problem I needed to work on for him was his stomach muscles which he tended to strain from time to time. So I used therapeutic ultra-sound treatment for heat before he played and then ice packs for twenty minutes afterwards. Apart from this little weakness he had good core strength and responded well to treatment. Bjorn was the quiet man of the tour. He never complained and just got on with his job of winning tennis matches which he did rather well!

A coach's job was rather more complicated politically, if not technically, than mine. I was employed by the ATP with a remit to treat all players equally, without regard to ranking and this I tried to do without offering any hint that I might warm to some more than others. But for a coach who is hired by a player rather than a tennis federation, life was a little more difficult, or, one might say, delicate. A coach in tennis is being paid by the man or woman to whom he has to give orders and if necessary, kick up the backside. How hard and how often do those kicks have to be administered before the player says, "Hey, buddy, enough of that. You're fired!"

So the coach, to varying degrees depending on the strength of his or her relationship, is walking on egg shells. First and foremost the coach needs the player to be winning. And it is tempting, if the player is in good form and progressing promisingly through a tournament, to want to overlook a potentially serious injury. They want that player on court, earning more points and more money – especially the latter because many coaches work on a small base salary with lots of bonus add-ons for winning titles or reaching finals. But, if they push too hard and the player breaks down, he's off the tour and no one is earning a cent because unlike athletes in team sports, pro tennis players have no guaranteed contracts. If they don't play, they don't earn.

Obviously, there were times when I felt I had to step in and say, "This guy needs a rest otherwise you are going to lose him for weeks." Timing is everything in sport, as in life, and one instance when it worked out perfectly was in 1999 when Andre Agassi strained the Pectoralis muscle in his serving shoulder. It happened at the ATP's World Team Cup in Dusseldorf, a special event which used to run every year a week before the French Open. I felt that rest and intensive special treatment were the only things that could get him fit for Roland Garros so I spoke to his coach Brad Gilbert and said it was imperative that Andre rest for a few days. Although time was short, Andre elected to fly back to his home in Las Vegas where his strength coach, Gil Reyes, took over and after some proper remedial work, sent him back to Paris. I wasn't convinced he was 100% fit by the time play started at Roland Garros but these top athletes continually surprise you with their resilience and their recovery speed. The break he had taken had done the trick. The muscles had recovered sufficiently to get him through the first few rounds and then, to many people's surprise – not least

Andre's – he went on to win the one Grand Slam title he had always felt offered him the greatest challenge. By beating Andrei Medvedev in the final, Agassi completed his quartet of Grand Slam titles, becoming only the fifth player in history after Fred Perry, Don Budge, Rod Laver and Roy Emerson to win all four in their careers. Since then, Roger Federer and Rafael Nadal have joined that select group and when you think of the great names who have not achieved it, one can understand why Andre is so proud to have done so.

It's frequently a judgment call as to whether a player is fit to walk on court. Fans who are critical of a player's performance, on a particular day, should realize that practically no one goes out there absolutely free of a little strain or pain – a little niggle as we call it. The game is simply too physical now to avoid stretching, pulling or tweaking a muscle or a ligament and one has to decide just how bad it is. Hard courts have exacerbated the problem over the past three decades, along with the ever growing power and speed of the athletes themselves.

In the days when the legendary Harry Hopman ran Australia's incredibly successful Davis Cup team, 'Hop' was able to put his players through all sorts of agony on court and off, partially because they were playing virtually all their tennis on grass or clay, surfaces that are much more forgiving on the body. Hopman had Stan Nicholes, an Olympic weight lifter who ran a gym in Melbourne, to help him and despite the fact that they frequently kept nocturnal hours which would make the modern day coach become faint, the game has known few fitter players than Frank Sedgman, Lew Hoad or Roy Emerson. Two- on- one drills under a burning Australian sun were just part of the routine. Nicholes said he never managed to find a physical task that Hoad could not accomplish while Emerson's muscles were made of steel as a result of all the work he did with push-ups and wall pulleys. People have asked me over the years how Emmo managed to win as many titles as he did while drinking as much beer as he did! Well, getting up at dawn – he never seemed to get a hangover – and running it all out of his system was the way it seemed to work for this ever cheerful personality.

Of course, they got hurt occasionally – although I am not sure little Ken Rosewall ever did – but, apart from Hoad's chronic back problem, they all stayed remarkably fit throughout long careers. And they all lived up to the Aussie creed: "If you walk on court, you're fit. No excuses." That sort of attitude helped make Rod Laver, Fred Stolle, Mal Anderson, John Newcombe, Tony Roche and their aforementioned colleagues some of the most popular people ever to have played the game. Apart from those periods when they were on Davis Cup duty with Hopman, they did not travel with a coach, which made for a level of camaraderie which is very difficult to replicate today when every top player is surrounded by an entourage of coaches, trainers, managers and publicity agents.

In one unique instance many of those jobs were carried out by one man – Ion Tiriac. The great Romanian with the droopy moustache and black hair that resembled coiled wire, had started his sporting career as a boxer and ice hockey player (of Olympic standard) and then, picking up a tennis racket, discovered he could frighten people with that, too. Tiriac was not a pretty or particularly skilled player but he was mighty effective and after trying to tame the wilder instincts of his young and impossibly talented compatriot Ilie Nastase, he started coaching seriously when he hooked up with Guillermo Vilas as his own playing career wound down.

The relationship between Tiriac and Vilas was one of the most extraordinary I have ever witnessed. Vilas was a very intelligent young man who used to write poetry and enjoyed music. But on a tennis court he was a stevedore and wanted to be worked like one. What he wanted was someone to run his life for him so that all he needed to worry about was getting the ball over the net. And that is what Tiriac did. He told the young Argentine what time to get up and when to go to bed; what and when to eat; when and how long to practice. Vilas didn't even want to know how much Tiriac earned from the exhibitions and contracts that Ion worked out for him. He just asked for a certain sum of money to be deposited in his bank account at year's end and whatever Tiriac made for himself was fine with Vilas. And for years it worked like a dream. Vilas became the world's second best clay court player after Bjorn Borg and won the French and Australian Opens. And he did it because his coach/manager/mentor was there with him morning, noon and night, looking after every detail. And that included how many shirts Guillermo took on court with him because he sweated more than any player I have known. Cliff Richey and Patrick Rafter sweated buckets on court but Vilas was in a class of his own and needed to change shirts all the time.

The relationship continued until a friend of Ion's from their boyhood days in Romania named Gunther Bosch called up Tiriac one day and told him about a young red head he was coaching in Germany named Boris Becker. Instantly recognizing his potential, Tiriac became Becker's manager and his relationship with Vilas started to peter out – rather too soon for Guillermo's liking, I believe.

By his looks as much as anything, Tiriac frightened a lot of people and in the beginning I found him a challenge. No question, he was tough. But, being very intelligent, he was prepared to listen and learn and after a while I found him terrific to deal with. Building a relationship with characters like Tiriac requires patience. It takes time. You must never adopt an attitude of being all-knowing. You have to sweeten the deal a little bit, explaining why, for instance, it is to their benefit that a player should rest or spend some time on the treatment table instead of the practice court. These guys are pro-active types who think that nothing is happening unless their guy is out there hitting balls. But it's really worth the extra effort to talk them through it and once a coach and trainer are working in harmony, the benefits to the player can be enormous.

Tiriac had a way about him that enabled him to get through to people like Nastase and later, Henri Leconte, the amusing but ill-disciplined Frenchman who had always been too much for the French Federation to handle. Ion never stood on ceremony and told it to you straight. He surrounded himself with advisers and was always ready to listen to anyone who had something sensible to say. Although his negotiating tactics were said to be outrageous, more often than not he got the best deal going and of course, ended up as a huge entrepreneur. Now one of the richest men in Romania, Tiriac owns car dealerships, TV and radio stations and until he sold it, a bank. He is also the chairman of the ATP Masters Series in Madrid and was instrumental in getting the city to build the futuristic Caja Majica – a magic box that contains three stadiums, all with sliding roofs. In all of our dealings he was always as good as his word. He is quite a character.

Bob Brett has always been another highly intelligent coach who has established his reputation as one of the best in the business through self-education. Brett, who grew up in Melbourne, was a pupil of the legendary Harry Hopman and under-pinned all his teachings with a strong work ethic. Small in stature but big on ideas, Brett has taken charge of an amazing number of player's careers over the years, beginning with the group sponsored by the ski company Rossignol who began making tennis rackets back in the seventies. Tim Mayotte, Andres Gomez, Tim Wilkison and Johan Kriek were members of that group and they all learned a lot from Brett even though he was still developing himself. After helping Paul McNamee and John Lloyd, he established himself in the top tier by taking charge of Boris Becker's career after Boris split with Bosch. In came Andrei Medvedev and Goran Ivanisevic. As Goran will tell you, it was not just tennis that you learned with Bob. He would add little history lessons about the places the tour visited and generally tried to broaden the player's horizons. Later Bob formed a productive partnership with another Croat, Marin Cilic and is now with the LTA in London.

I watched Larry Stefanki transform himself from a feisty, aggressive player into one of the world's top coaches, cutting his teeth by helping John McEnroe towards the end of John's career – not the easiest way to begin but they had always been good friends on the tour. Then, as Larry and I developed a good rapport, he switched to Patrick McEnroe. As an example of the way an athletic trainer can help out, Stefanki came to me one day and asked if I had noticed that Patrick was starting his matches slowly, especially on the serve. I said I had and that it was probably as a result of tension and muscle stiffness. So we started giving Patrick's shoulder extra attention with manual therapy and exercises before his matches and it helped. The solution is not rocket science but often the way to go about it requires cooperation because you will never have the chance to get to the player if his coach does not fit the time for treatment into his pre-match routine.

Stefanki, who is a great talker and motivator although he would appear quiet and introverted on first meeting, went on to handle two of the more difficult characters on the tour and was amazingly successful. The truculent Chilean, Marcelo Rios, was not the most popular guy around but he was supremely talented and Larry helped the little left hander reach No 1 in the world although he never managed to win a Grand Slam. Then he took on Yevgeny Kafelnikov and helped the Russian win his second Slam at the Australian Open in 1999 and get to the final again in Melbourne the following year when he lost to Andre Agassi. These guys were very different types but they both posed a challenge to a coach who, as I have mentioned, is in that delicate position of wondering just how far he can push a guy before the player rebels and kicks him out. Stefanki earned the respect of these two difficult personalities because he is a motivator who knows what he is talking about. Later the much more amenable Tim Henman and Francisco Gonzalez both found this to be true and until he finally called it quits, Larry kept Andy Roddick on the road as that great American warrior battled through the aches and pains that come from staying at the top of the game for over ten years.

The aches and pains may vary in intensity but, believe me, they are always there. It really comes down to a player's pain threshold and how much of it he can endure. When I am asked about players who could tolerate a high level of pain, I immediately think of Boris Becker, Jimmy Connors, Arthur Ashe, Rod Laver and Michael Chang and perhaps most of all, Luke Jensen who won the French Open doubles title with his brother Murphy in 1993. Luke, who was one of that rare breed, a totally ambidextrous player who frequently switched from serving righty or lefty in the middle of a game, used to suffer terribly from pain in his knees but he always had a grin on his face and just got on with it.

Because he was not the complaining type, few people realized how much pain Ashe suffered from a calcaneal bone spur in his heel. This is the bone that attaches to the Achilles and when it is irritated like Arthur's frequently was, it feels as if you are walking on a thousand tin tacks. He wore those Dutch-style clogs which have no back to free him of some of the pain but it was an on-going problem for him. Like the others I have mentioned, Ashe was strong enough mentally to just block it out. There is no cookbook on this; the recipe lies in the player's head and whatever message he manages to send to his nerve ends.

Some just feel it more than most because everyone's different. Gene Mayer, who had as much touch with his two handed game as anyone I have ever seen, found it difficult to play through pain as did the great Italian champion Adriano Panatta who was always coming to me to have something done about the blisters that frequently appeared on the heel of his racket hand. Bjorn Borg often had the same problem but he just asked for tape and did the job himself. Panatta needed help but it is very difficult to get adhesive tape to stay in place. The tape migrates with the movement that takes place every time you hit the ball. We were always struggling to get Adriano properly bandaged.

Discovering a player's pain threshold and working out ways of dealing with whatever problems it throws up is something that coaches and athletic trainers need to work on together because some of it becomes psychological. Will a kick in the pants work? Probably not but sometimes it is worth a try!

Chapter 6: John McEnroe

I think I still have a good relationship with John McEnroe because I was always honest with him and never accepted the worst excesses of his frequently appalling behavior. Yes, we did have our moments.

It is not good enough to brand McEnroe a brat any more than passing him off as a great guy would do justice to this incredibly complex human being. He can be rude and courteous; compassionate, caring and hugely generous as well as abrupt and forgetful. His mind is as sharp as a razor and he possesses a good sense of humor as those who have become fans of his television commentating have come to realize. But the simmering temper can explode at any moment and his performances on the ATP Champions tour these days are often marred by a foul mouthed tirade. In his younger days I don't think he could help himself and was often regretful afterwards. Now I think he believes that a blow -out is what is expected of him, indeed what he is paid for, but sometimes he still loses control. So it is not always an act.

I was working the ATP Champions tour event at Delray Beach recently and as always, he brought the crowds in. But by the time he had played a couple of matches, some of the older patrons were muttering about his abusive language and denouncing him as a disgrace. It has always been that way. Some people will tolerate it and others won't. At 55, he still plays with lots of pride, and expects the chair umpire and the line judges to give their best efforts as well. He busts his butt on the court and he expects everyone that is involved in the match to bust their butts as well.

There were times on the tour early in his career when I stepped in and told him to get a grip of himself. There was the occasion at a Davis Cup tie in Cincinnati when he went berserk at a cameraman who was shooting courtside. McEnroe shoved the camera so hard back into the man's face that the poor guy had rivulets of blood running down from his forehead.

"What the hell do you think you are doing?" I yelled at him. "The guy's doing his job! You have no right to behave like that."

I believe incidents like that brought an early end to Tony Trabert's reign as Davis Cup captain. Trabert was one of the great American champions who won Wimbledon as well as the French title at Roland Garros and being a patriot, took great pride in captaining his country's Davis Cup team. He also formed a very close relationship with McEnroe and offered the hugely talented young man all sorts of sound advice that helped him maximize those talents. But even Trabert could not control McEnroe once he got on court.

In 1980, we were playing Mexico in the Davis Cup at Chapultapec Park and despite the fact that the US had established a 2-0 winning lead after the first two days, McEnroe said things to the Mexican captain, Yves Lemaitre, no one should ever say.

We spoke to Trabert about that tie recently and after confirming that he did, indeed, decide to step down because of what happened in Mexico City, he went on to recall the events this way:

"John and Vitas Gerulaitis had won the two opening singles pretty easily against Raul Ramirez and Marcello Lara and then, on the Saturday, John and Peter Fleming took the first two sets of the doubles 6-3, 6-3. Then, suddenly, Fleming lost his serve in the third and McEnroe starting trying to drive volleys all over the place and lost his, too. We lost that set 12-10 and the fourth as well. At the change over I asked them if they wanted to play like pros or go on playing like jerks. Fleming took offense at that and said they didn't want to play for a captain who abused them. I said, 'OK, I'll take you off court then and we'll default the tie.' That calmed them down and they started playing properly again.

"Everything seemed under control at match point, 5-2 in the fifth, Ramirez serving at 0-40 when McEnroe suddenly calls out, 'You foot faulted!' Their captain, Yves Lemaitre, jumped out his chair in fury and McEnroe went over to him, calling him names. I got in between them, asking McEnroe how the hell he could make a call on a line at the other end of the court but by then the crowd were into it and started throwing cushions. One of them hit our sponsor, Byron Radaker of Congoleum, who told me later he did not want to sponsor anything that embarrassed him. And it was embarrassing. The security people kept us in the little locker room for an hour after the match because they told us there were some pretty angry people outside. Hardly surprising! The whole thing was ridiculous and as usual with John, so unnecessary. I decided I'd had enough."

Trabert went on to recount how the incident came up again at an 80th birthday party that was laid on for him at the 21 Club in Manhattan just recently. "John spoke at the dinner and actually apologized for his behavior in Mexico City. He knew it had caused my resignation because I had told him some years before when he asked about it but at least he eventually got around to saying sorry!"

The fact that McEnroe attended the dinner shows just how much respect he maintained for Trabert and that was as it should be because Tony bore no grudges and continued to help John tactically on occasion. I saw evidence of it when Trabert walked into the No 1 locker room at Wimbledon – as an honorary member of the All England Club he had carte blanche to go where he pleased – and sat down with John an hour or so before he was due to face Jimmy Connors in the 1984 final. "Yes, that's true," said Trabert. "I spoke to John before the match and suggested he served more into Jimmy's body to stop him taking a swing at those serves. His return was only effective when he could free his arms. I think it helped stifle Connors that day because McEnroe played brilliantly. It tends to get forgotten as a match because it was so one sided. People only remember the epic five setters but the quality of tennis John produced in that final was extraordinary. It's not easy to beat Connors 6-1, 6-1, 6-2."

The fact that Trabert was prepared to do that says a great deal about how people who really know John feel about him. Most of us, I think, see so much good in the guy that we are much more prepared to cut him some slack than those who only watch him from afar or may, unhappily, have been the recipient of his foul temper.

It's a fact of human nature that personalities like McEnroe create headlines and attract more attention than a well-behaved performer. To that extent, McEnroe, Connors and Ilie Nastase must be credited with fueling the tennis boom that took hold, especially in America, in the seventies. Obviously there was a negative aspect to their antics because much of it was X-rated but they brought the crowds in and tennis became a far bigger attraction, especially on television, than it had ever been.

The problem, of course, was keeping the cap on the worst blow outs. Back in the seventies and eighties umpires and officials were not nearly as professional as they are now and some of the nice gentleman who took on the onerous task of officiating top flight matches at Wimbledon and elsewhere were simply not experienced enough to handle the job. McEnroe has admitted that it might have done him good to be thrown off court early in his career. "It might have taught me a lesson," he has told my co-author Richard Evans.

I seem to remember that it was Wing Commander George Grime and Edward James who took the brunt of McEnroe's abuse at Wimbledon in the early years. Neither of these two generally excellent umpires, nor referee Fred Hoyles, was prepared to declare a default. Poor Fred, he was a gentleman farmer from Lincolnshire and nothing during his peaceful existence had prepared him to having to deal with this screaming, curly-headed kid from New York with his red headband and scabrous phraseology of which "You Cannot Be Serious!" became the most famous, partially because it could be quoted in front of one's grandmother. Hoyles had to listen to too much that wasn't. But, generally, he dealt with the eruptions pretty well and kept the show on the road which was, of course, what the public and TV executives wanted. It is a cynical but undeniable fact that major draw cards are no use to anyone if they are not allowed to play.

It was not until 1990 that the British umpire Gerry Armstrong, now one of the world's most experienced and respected officials, called referee Ken Farrar on court at the Australian Open and having already penalized the American for racket abuse, gave McEnroe his marching orders after another foul-mouthed tirade directed at Farrar as he was about to leave the court. "Even if Ken had not heard what McEnroe called him, I would have de-faulted him anyway because I heard it," Armstrong said afterwards. "Abuse of that kind should be an immediate default offense." If only officials like Armstrong and Farrar had been around a decade earlier! But by then it was all a bit late and all John accomplished was to ruin his chance of grabbing another Grand Slam title because he had been playing brilliantly at Melbourne Park that year and was leading the Swede, Mikael Pernfors, by two sets to one in the fourth round. Any chance of lessons being learned was long gone.

Interestingly, very little of McEnroe's invective was directed across the net at his opponents. Occasionally, however, a player would get the benefit of the New Yorker's sarcastic sense of humor. It happened to Boris Becker one year at the Paris Indoors. The German had developed a cough which might have become a trifle psychosomatic because it usually erupted at critical moments in a match. Boris made John wait to receive serve because of it and when Boris held up his hand to apologize, saying, "Sorry I have this cough," McEnroe shot back, "God, you've had it a long time then!"

But although nearly all his histrionics were directed at court officials, that did not mean to say that McEnroe's behavior did not impact his opponents. Frequently, it used to drive them nuts because it broke their concentration and interrupted the flow of the match.

There was one memorable incident during the Milan Indoors which was played at the Palazzo dello Sport – a building with a lovely curved, concave roof which unhappily did not survive a heavy snow fall a couple of years later. The design might have been aesthetically pleasing, but the weight of the snow proved too much for it and the roof fell in. Some would say that it should have fallen on McEnroe's head, considering the mayhem he had caused beneath it, and Steve Denton and Kevin Curren would probably agree.

Denton and Curren were one of the best doubles teams of their generation and were often locked in deadly battles with McEnroe and his long-time partner Peter Fleming. However, on this occasion, I think John was playing with his good buddy from New York, Peter Rennert, and McEnroe's antics had finally gone too far for Denton, a massive and normally genial Texan we called "Bull". On returning to the locker room after the match, Denton grabbed McEnroe by the throat and had him up against the wall. Curren, a lean, steely-eyed South African who had quite a short fuse himself, looked as if he might join in and I thought I had better do something before my work load was increased by the need to   patch up combatants. Before stopping to think what the consequences might be, I flung myself in between Denton and McEnroe and yelled at them to stop it. Come to think of it, perhaps that's why John and I are still friends. Maybe, he thinks I saved his life!

I had first gotten to know the kid from Douglaston, New York when he was a ball boy at Forest Hills in the seventies. The US Open was still being played at the West Side Tennis Club where I worked out of a corner room in the old clubhouse up on the third floor. There were, of course, scores of ball boys running around during the tournament but John tended to catch the eye because he was buzzing about everywhere and showing what he could do with a racket in his hand whenever he could grab time on court. His wood racket – the old Jack Kramer Pro or later the Dunlop Maxply – just seemed like an extension of his hand so complete was his mastery of the ball.

His talents were quickly recognized and along with Larry Gottfried and Van Winitsky, I remember him being attached to the Davis Cup squad we took down to Chile when he was still relatively unknown. His enthusiasm for the Davis Cup had been instilled into him by his parents who had taught him that there was no greater honor than to represent your country and it was a lesson he took to heart. In between listening to Meat Loaf on his tapes, John was ready to muck in on court and off and even later when he became the star of the team, he was always – to some people's disbelief – a great team man. Especially on Davis Cup duty he was always ready to step up and play, and if Vitas Gerulaitis was on the squad, the pair of them used to have a great time. But he was not much of a role model as far as organization with clothes and equipment was concerned. Clothes for the day tended to be plucked out of his huge Nike bag and sniffed to determine their level of hygiene. In sharp contrast to what he expected of himself on court, the standards required in this department were not too high!

One could almost gauge the amount of sheer natural ability he possessed by the fact that he didn't train very hard and tended to use his doubles matches with Fleming to iron out any kinks in his game. Amazingly he did not have a great range of motion and was certainly not as supple as someone like Nastase. Adrenaline flowed through his body like an electric current and it all came out through those magical hands. Early on he had very few injuries and I rarely had to do much for him other than offer manual therapy on his lower back and forearm – and help him stretch.

Inevitably that started to change by the time he reached his mid-twenties and the thought finally dawned on him that a little extra training might be necessary. He actually went as far as equipping his Malibu beach house with a gym, complete with wall climber, and slowly started to take greater care of his body. The transformation in recent years has been startling. With all the lingering baby fat long gone, McEnroe has turned himself into one of the fittest fifty-something athletes in the world. His competitive instincts are such that, when faced with reality, he has become more than willing to run the extra mile so that he can stay fit enough to confront players like Goran Ivanisevic and Mark Philippoussis on the ATP Champions tour – opponents twenty years his junior. In some ways, John could now act as a poster boy for this book because there could be few finer examples of how to do the right things in order to remain competitive in middle age.

Everyone who knows him personally recognizes that there is so much good in the guy and it is a crying shame that the general public will probably remember him for the dark side of his personality. But that does not properly reflect the real man. It would be impossible to find a more loyal friend and he has never forgotten his roots. His schoolboy pals from Douglaston, New York are still his pals and we will never know how many people have received the benefit of John's largesse when it comes to helping those in need financially. I can assure you it is a large number.

He may not like everything I have written in this chapter but he has always been honest about himself and he will recognize that I am just being honest here. It is typical of the man that he immediately agreed to write a forward to this book. He never forgets his friends and I am proud to call myself one of them.

Chapter 7: Arthur Ashe

I want to talk for a moment about Arthur Ashe because, as I am sure most people understand by now, he was special. Emotionally, Arthur had a wonderful heart; medically he had a terrible heart. It was hereditary and it led to him having bi-pass surgery at the age of thirty-six which seemed ridiculous, really, because you wouldn't have found a leaner, cleaner living athlete.

But he kept a lot of his emotions bottled up inside which is never a good thing and then, as if one heart surgery wasn't enough, he received a second bi-pass heart surgery in 1983. There he received an infusion of contaminated blood at a New York hospital which gave him the HIV. He died at age 49.

His reaction to the terrible hand that fate had dealt him was so typical and so revealing of the man. When asked if he ever thought why he, Arthur Ashe, with so much to live for and so much still to do, had been hit with this death sentence, he replied, "Do I ever think 'Why me?' No. Why, not me?"

Arthur and I became friends very early on because, I suppose, I understood where he was coming from. I had grown up in the south as a white boy and had seen, close up, what segregation meant in America in the fifties. In Fort Myers, Florida, a sunny place by the sea, the dark forces of prejudice were part of my daily life. African-Americans had different swimming pools and different toilets and they had their own restaurants. Water fountains and restrooms were designated White or Colored. You know, it never seemed right to me.

This attempt at enforcing segregation continued on through the sixties by which time I was working for the New York Mets baseball club. We were on a bus trip once that was taking us from Columbus, Georgia all the way up to Auburn, New York. By the time we hit Augusta, we decided to stop at a restaurant for something to eat. Three of our team members were African-

American and the restaurant refused to serve them. So it was back on the bus until we found a place that would serve us all.

Arthur and I swapped stories like this as we got to know each other – me, relatively new to tennis after my time in other sports and him new to the whole white world. Arthur had been brought up by a strict but loving father in Richmond, Virginia and had then moved to Lynchburg under the care of Dr. Robert Johnson, a tennis teacher and educator who instilled in Arthur the creed which enabled him to become accepted so quickly once he joined the tour. "Never give the white man an excuse to criticize you. Rise above any prejudice you might find. You are better than that."

Arthur was well disposed to listen to this advice because his father had laid the groundwork. "What people think of you, Arthur Junior, is your reputation, that's all that counts."

Arthur's dignified bearing and refusal to react to any slight he might encounter – not to mention the thrilling way he hit a tennis ball – enabled him to become a popular member of the tennis community very quickly. But it was a double edged sword because, in the days of the Black Panthers and other militants, Arthur was viewed as not being radical enough. But, slowly, over time the more impatient members of the black community came to understand that there are many ways to fight the good fight and that Arthur Ashe was fighting his corner pretty well.

Some people adopted Arthur's methods quicker than others and no one was more immediately perceptive about Arthur than the black South African poet Don Mattera who was unable to attend a meeting of black journalists that he had organized for Arthur on his first visit to South Africa in 1973 because, just a few days before, Mattera had been 'banned' by the apartheid government. That was the Nationalist Party's favorite ploy when they wanted to silence someone who was a nuisance. It meant that someone who had been 'banned' could not meet in public with more than one other person. So Mattera, shadowed by a BOSS agent, had to meet Arthur outside the hall and apologize for not being able to join him inside. There was a hilarious element to this because the government had gone to enormous pains to present the best side of their tortured nation to their celebrated visitor – Ashe's first visit after being denied a visa for years was headline news – and now they had taken careful aim and shot themselves in the foot. Mattera's banning order had been in the bureaucratic works and by chance and great ill timing, had been spewed out right in the middle of Arthur's visit.

But Mattera offered Arthur something better than merely accompanying him to a meeting. He wrote a wonderful poem about him which was so insightful and read, in part:

"Your youthful face

A mask

Hiding a pining, anguished spirit and

I loved you brother –

Not for your quiet philosophy

But for the rage in your soul

Trained to be rebuked or summoned."

This was the essence of Arthur Ashe, captured so brilliantly by Mattera who had hardly met him.

By the time he won Wimbledon in 1975, Ashe had risen above the status of being just another fine tennis pro. He had become a leader in every sense. He was at the heart of the formation of the Association of Tennis Professionals (ATP) in 1972; was deeply involved in the decision to boycott Wimbledon in 1973 and was President of the ATP by the time he beat Jimmy Connors in that unforgettable final on the Centre Court.

The year 1975 was exceptional for Arthur. He had it all going for him that year. He did have tremendous stress on him but he was able to manage it. There were many times that year that he would come to me for my assistance. Somehow after doing some deep tissue work on his muscles there was a great release of tension. He was then able to relax and face another day, another opponent, and enjoy that wonderful season.

Once his playing career wound down, it was inevitable that Ashe would become America's Davis Cup captain. It was not an easy assignment and once again, he found himself blessed and cursed by fate. He took over the captaincy in the era of two of the country's most outstanding talents, McEnroe and Connors. That was the upside. The downside came with McEnroe's frequently appalling behavior – which appalled no one more than Ashe himself – and Connors' reluctancy to play on a team. McEnroe was a team player and Jimmy preferred to play for himself.

Ashe finished with a record of 13 wins and 3 defeats, including two Cup winning years in 1981 and 1982. But the effort would have tested the stamina of a fully healthy man, let alone one who had undergone heart surgery in 1979 and needed a double by-pass in 1983. Obviously, as trainer to the Davis Cup squad, I took Arthur's state of health very seriously and was never more concerned than during the disastrous Davis Cup final of 1984 in Gothenburg when Sweden humiliated a star-studded American team that should have done so much better.

As Arthur admitted in his book "Days of Grace" it turned out to be "one of the most dismal points of my tennis career". For various reasons, McEnroe and Connors arrived late; Connors left an obscene note for Ashe and Jimmy Arias because they were 15 minutes behind schedule for a practice session and then, in a year when McEnroe had been virtually invincible, the little known Henrik Sundstrom beat John quite easily after Mats Wilander had destroyed Connors on the specially laid clay court.

With team members who either hated each other or felt intimidated by the star power of the top two, Arthur was juggling practice times and generally walking on egg shells.

The stress was considerable and whenever I could, I grabbed him for a few minutes to try and relieve the knot in his taut shoulders and neck muscles, which were like boards, with deep tissue therapy and some manual therapy. That offered only temporary relief. Through it all, I was worried about his heart.

At all our Davis Cup ties, I arranged ahead of time for a cardiologist to be in the stadium. I had networked the medical world on a global basis pretty extensively during my travels so I could always find someone to call on, even if some were very reluctant to get involved because of possible litigation. I never told Arthur I was doing this but it became common practice for me to find pediatricians or gynecologists for those members of our team who travelled with wives and young families, like Marty Riessen and Hank Pfister. We were a family and I wanted to make sure everyone was taken care of.

Looking back to those years, Arthur suffered from hypertension. As much as we tried to relieve this condition, it was a day to day battle to help him. He put so much on his plate and was always trying to help people with their various problems. He was a rare person, always concerned about the less fortunate and trying to make a difference in many people's lives.

There is not a day that passes that I don't think about Arthur. I miss him terribly.

Chapter 8: Connors & Agassi

"Bill Norris is a man that with his hands could heal your body, but with his spirit, generosity and strength could heal the scars left on your soul from defeat and failure...a priceless gift to all athletes. He impacted me and countless others in ways he will never know."

— Andre Agassi

Jimmy Connors and Andre Agassi – two peas in a pod? It would have to be a rather strange pod but these two definitely spring from the same kind of vegetable. Andre was a very small pea, indeed, when his father turned up at the Pancho Gonzalez Pro Shop at Caesar's Palace in Las Vegas one day and virtually demanded that Pancho find someone to hit with his four year old son.

It was 1974 and the young man lounging in a chair after practice was on the brink of superstardom. Connors would win three Grand Slam titles that year and was already established as a cocky, combative player who knew what he wanted and where he was going. Jimmy didn't listen to many people other than his mother, his grandmother (Two Mom as he called her) and the fearsome Gonzalez who demanded respect, not just by his demeanor but as a result of his achievements as a leading light on the old Jack Kramer pro tour. So when Pancho turned to Jimmy, his eyes twinkling above the scar that ran down one side of his face, and said, "Jimbo, give this kid a hit" the only reaction he got from Connors other than immediate acquiescence was a look of disbelief.

So out they went, the swaggering top tenner and the tiny tot and started to hit balls. Gonzalez was not being completely frivolous. He already knew Mike Agassi because Andre's Dad worked as a casino captain for the shows at the MGM Grand in one of the casinos on the Strip and he had heard that the kid knew how to hit a ball. Mike Agassi also was a racket stringer and strung Connors rackets. But even he was surprised at just how well Andre managed to wield a racket that was not much smaller than himself. And so was Jimmy. "Kid's amazing," he muttered on returning to the shop. In one way or the other Andre Agassi has remained amazing throughout his life.

So the pair of them had this unlikely connection from very early on and in 1992, Connors made his last appearance at Wimbledon and lost in the first round. It was the year Agassi won the title. Amazing.

The connection was stronger than a mere chance meeting in Las Vegas. Of all the players I have been around over the past thirty odd years, these two were the most shut off and protective of their space as they prepared for a match. The intensity of their focus was unequalled by anyone I have ever known. Roger Federer and Rafael Nadal are extremely focused before their matches but both can be cordial to other people in the locker room in a distant sort of way. Heck, Andre didn't want to be in the locker room at all and often wasn't. Jimmy stayed in his corner, like a boxer preparing for a fight, surrounded only by those from his small, intimate circle like Lorne Kuhle and Doug Henderson.

Agassi was so keen on his privacy that he found other places to change before a match. At Roland Garros, before the players' area was re-built, there was a little room, not more than a cupboard, near where the athletic trainers worked and Agassi used to go and change in there. For a couple of years, Nike, his clothing company at the time, parked a mobile home on Avenue Gordon Bennett which runs down the side of the tennis complex in Paris and he used that as his private locker room.

With Andre, shyness was a factor but with both of them it was a lot more than that. They had been brought up by parents, Gloria Connors and Mike Agassi who taught them that an opponent was a foe; a man to be brought down; a man to whom no quarter should be given. The Texan, Cliff Richey, who was of Connors' generation, was the same. He worked up a hate against the person he was about to play. It didn't always get that personal with Connors and Agassi but anyone close to them in the draw; anyone they were likely to have to play that week, was lucky if they got so much as a nod of recognition. Want a smile and a hello? Forget it.

Neither was interested in being part of any kind of fraternity. Tennis is an individual sport and they liked it that way. Agassi managed to broaden his perspective while playing Davis Cup for the United States but Connors always struggled with the concept of having to support and worry about teammates.

For someone like me, who had come into the game in the era of the great Australians, this was a contrast that took a bit of getting used to. Rod Laver, Roy Emerson, Fred Stolle, John Newcombe, Tony Roche, Owen Davidson, Ray Ruffels, Dick Crealy and quite a few others were so close that they made that rule that I mentioned earlier: Anyone not present and correct at the hotel bar at 7.00 pm had to pay a fine. And that was just the start of the evening's festivities. They might have been bashing each other's brains out on court all afternoon but that highly competitive spirit was switched off the moment the match was over. They were mates. And to Australians, in particular, that means something special.

Dr. Allen Fox, a Davis Cup player and psychologist, will tell you that all top tennis players are inherently suspicious. The Australians, because of their environment and upbringing which teaches you to look after your mates no matter what, were probably less suspicious than most. But Connors and Agassi were more so. Connors, from a working class background in Illinois with a hugely competitive mother and Agassi, the son of an immigrant who boxed for Iran, were never taught to worry about anyone else except themselves. Connors took a long time to realize this wasn't a great way to live your life. Agassi, to his great credit, got the message earlier and has now helped change thousands of children's lives in Las Vegas with the creation of his charter school.

Both of them needed treatment from time to time; someone to turn to when they got hurt. More often than not, that was me. As you might have realized by now, I have been blessed with the kind of nature that instinctively wants to embrace people. I am, I suppose, a tolerant soul and prefer to search out the good in those I have to deal with. It is why I survived in the personality-driven atmosphere of a sporting locker room with all the different temperaments reacting to the extreme stresses of competition. If: Triumph and disaster – treat those two imposters just the same? Really? Kipling was asking for a lot. At any given moment during my day on tour I could have Eddie Dibbs running around like a banshee, cracking jokes and creating happy mayhem as he worked off his nerves before a match or Bob Hewitt threatening to punch someone out after a loss. Others would brood in stony silence or cry in a corner. Some would want to pick through every detail of their match as they lay on my treatment table. I would have to be all things to all people. It was my job.

It could also have lost me my job as far as my relationship with Connors was concerned. I had known him since he first burst onto the tour as an unconstructed young kid of seventeen. I saw where he was coming from because Gloria was always there and she was one tough lady. But I established a good relationship with her and Jimmy and I never had any real problems. But then everything started to get political.

Connors, being a maverick, proved easy pickings for Bill Riordan, an extraordinary character from Salisbury, Maryland whose brother, incidentally, ended up as Mayor of Los Angeles. Riordan was a go-getter and hugely ambitious. He got a license from the USTA to start an indoor circuit soon after Open Tennis came into being in 1968 and he ran it his way. No matter what your standard was, you got into a Riordan tournament if he liked you. If not, forget it. He was a genial, persuasive sort of guy and cunning as a cat. He knew who sold tickets and he didn't care how they did it. So Connors and the combustible Romanian star Ilie Nastase became his favorites. He paid them whatever it took to play his tournaments and for a few years, the Riordan circuit was a big success at cities along the Eastern seaboard.

Riordan had bigger ideas. As soon as the Association of Tennis Professionals (ATP) was formed in 1972, he thought, "Why can't I do that?" And so he tried. He signed up Connors and said that Nastase and a dozen other players had preferred to join his Independent Players Association rather than the ATP. Later when he was forced to open his books this turned out to be untrue. The only signed up members of his association were Connors, his lawyer and himself. Rather sad, really.

In the meantime, things started to get nasty – a lot nastier than Ilie. When the ATP objected to his pronouncements, Connors sued not only the organization but Arthur Ashe, who was President at the time, personally. So the two Wimbledon finalists of 1975 – the year Ashe beat Connors so dramatically – were actually in litigation against each other as they walked out onto Centre Court.

And in the middle of all this was me. My problem was that I was employed by the ATP but had been looking after Jimmy ever since he joined the tour. And not only was Jimmy not an ATP member but he was suing them! I suppose I could have turned round and said, "Sorry, son, go somewhere else for your therapy." But that's not how I like to deal with people so we had to get a little discreet. On occasion, we would sneak off to someone's apartment near the courts or go back to the hotel. After a while some of the ATP officials realized what was going on but no one ever called me on it. I spoke to Jim McManus, a great guy and former player who devoted his life to the ATP, about the Connors problem and said, "Listen Jim, Connors may be suing the ATP but he's still playing our tournaments. He's the biggest draw card in the game and just by playing he's making the tour money. If he can't get treatment when he plays our events, he's a big enough star to go and play exhibitions. Then everyone loses. Cut us some slack."

McManus was close to Bob Briner, the Texan who took over as CEO of the ATP Tour from Jack Kramer in the mid-seventies and as I never heard from the boss on the subject, everything worked out just fine. As for the law suit, I think it was settled out of court and a sort of an uneasy truce pervaded the tour as far as Connors and his fellow players were concerned. At least until John McEnroe arrived on the scene. But that's another story.

The bottom line as far as Connors, Nastase, McEnroe and Agassi is concerned is that they, possibly more than any other players, took the game of tennis out of the country clubs and made it a sport that attracted the average sports nut. They broadened its appeal; got people through the turnstiles and made it so big that, today, 720,000 tickets are sold for the US Open. They did it by virtue of their incredible skill; amazing dedication to their profession and their unique, tempestuous and frequently over-the-top personalities. There have been other great stars over the years, coming from all walks of life and all corners of the globe but this quartet, I feel, are a breed apart.

Whether Nastase and McEnroe fit so snugly into the Connors-Agassi pod is debatable but there are genes there that would certainly recognize each other. But are they compatible? No, that's my territory. I just tried to keep the peace.

I do know that Connors and Agassi provided some great moments on the courts. I never saw anyone ever play with as much desire and pure blood and guts as Connors did. Jimmy fought you with everything he had even if he had to spill his blood on the court to do it.

Agassi always found a way to beat his opponent. Andre continued to re-invent himself as his career progressed. He possessed great court sense and always worked on his game to improve.

Both were great showmen, crowd pleasers, ticket sellers, headline makers and as a result, great assets to the game of tennis. I was very fortunate to work with these two champions.

Chapter 9: Ivan Lendl

A lot of players hide their true personalities on court. As I have said, my near neighbor in Boca Raton, Chris Evert, was one. Little Miss Ice Maiden never did let her wicked sense of humor leak out during matches.

But the public were probably fooled to an even greater extent by Ivan Lendl. You would have thought that, after taking American citizenship and proceeding to establish the quite incredible record of reaching eight consecutive US Open finals, Ivan would have forged some kind of rapport with his public. But Old Stone Face never let them in. Those who have never spent time with Ivan would not believe what an extrovert he really is. He is a non-stop story teller with an unending stream of jokes, most of which would make people's hair curl. His line of humor is, you might say, indelicate and would certainly not be to everyone's taste. But he is funny and has a very good mind. When you had him on the treatment table, you found yourself discussing world politics – not a topic that was rife in most locker rooms I worked in.

He was also a prankster par excellence and no one was safe with Ivan around. Just ask the Wimbledon doubles champion, Bob Hewitt. Or given the South African's temper, maybe not! Anyway Hewitt was the victim of one of Lendl's more extravagant pranks. One year at Wimbledon, Hewitt decided he wanted a nap and lay down on one of the treatment tables. Bob was a good sleeper and was soon soundly in dream land. Lendl spotted this and decided he would make sure Hewitt would get a really good rest! Seizing a great roll of the plastic wrap we use to tape up shoulders and elbows, Ivan proceeded to mummify Hewitt with it, running the tape under the table and all over Bob's body. With his arms pinned to his sides, Bob was completely immobilized when he woke up and was, as you can imagine, fit to burst. Ivan was in hysterics.

You had to stand up to Lendl if you wanted to get the best of him; goad him a little bit; show him you were ready for a little sparring. Ivan and his great friend Warren Bosworth, a technical expert who looked after Lendl's rackets and equipment, were always going at each with a non-stop series of biting barbs which would have offended a lot of people. But they loved it and Ivan was devastated when Warren passed away in the fall of 2010.

I would tease Ivan about his weight – he put on a huge amount after he retired – and we always had a good relationship, which was lucky because he didn't always take it kindly when someone tried to turn the tables on him. One who succeeded was Murphy Jensen, a familiar figure now on Tennis Channel with his travel programs, and the brother of Luke with whom he won the French Open in 1993.

We were at the ECC tournament in Antwerp where they used to give a diamond studded racket to the winner. Ivan won it more than once if I remember correctly. Anyway, it was a winter tournament and it was snowing outside as Lendl came for his massage and then went for a nice long shower. Murphy had been preparing for this and as soon as Lendl was stark naked, he nipped behind him and took all his street clothes – underpants, jeans, jacket, all his clothes – and stuffed them in the freezer. When Lendl emerged from the shower a great roar went up. "Where are my clothes? Who's the bastard who's stolen my clothes! Bill? Who was it?"

I put on a deadpan look of blissful innocence but Murphy, who was lucky to escape with his life, was soon uncovered as the culprit. Murphy had the last laugh. When Ivan's clothes were retrieved from the freezer, they were stiff as boards – and not very nice to wear on a cold night!

Mind you, Lendl did not balk at putting his body through hardship. He would look at himself in the mirror on the morning of a training day and say, "Now, Body! How much can I make you suffer today?" If you detect a streak of masochism there then I suppose Ivan was guilty as far as punishing himself in training was concerned. I worked with a lot of fit athletes – Brian Gottfried worked as hard as anyone, as did

Jim Courier and the Englishman Roger Taylor who always kept very fit back in the days when the levels weren't quite the same as they are today. Even earlier, there was Roy Emerson, a superb athlete who was probably the fittest of a very fit bunch of Australian stars all trained by the legendary Harry Hopman who honed them on his two-on-one practice sessions and kangaroo jumps. Hopman was assisted in this by Stan Nicholes, a former Olympic weight lifter who, later, helped Chris Evert bulk up so that she could withstand the challenge of the increasingly fit and athletic Martina Navratilova. I would still put Lendl in a class of his own.

He was an innovator, too, bringing new methods of strengthening exercises to the tour. He was the first to utilize mountain bikes and the rather more exotic idea of running with a small weighted parachute strapped to his back to increase wind resistance. His zeal was quite incredible and he was always tinkering with new ideas to build on the explosive power he developed as a result of his efforts.

On being asked once what he did for relaxation after all his physical effort, Ivan replied, "I go and wrestle the dogs!". As the dogs were five rather fierce German Shepherds, most of which he bought as puppies from the Czech border guards and trained himself, Ivan's idea of 'relaxation' was hardly akin to reading a book by the fire. When Lendl had his coach, Tony Roche, staying with him at his home in Connecticut, Tony would sit nervously in the kitchen at breakfast, keeping a wary eye on the hounds as they patrolled the house. "You know, Tony," Ivan would remind him somewhat needlessly, "they are all trained to react to the Czech word for 'Kill!'" Pete Sampras was another visitor who was scared witless by the dogs but no one ever got any sympathy from their master. It just fed Ivan's rather particular sense of humor.

I was never quite sure how Samantha survived all this. Ivan must be different with the women in his life – and he is not short of them. Having married Samantha, whose family owned the Caribbean resort, La Samanna, on St Martin, when she was still a teenager, this quiet, lovely girl proceeded to give him five daughters. That put a stop to his goading of guys on the tour, like John Fitzgerald, who had had daughters and no son. To the amusement of many, the great macho man found himself in a house full of women but he loved them all dearly and has been a wonderful father. Three of them picked up on his passion for golf – a sport he played to a high standard after retiring from tennis – and have become top class junior golfers themselves, thanks to their father's coaching and encouragement. For several years, Ivan would drive them from tournament to tournament up and down the eastern seaboard in his big brown van, staying at cheap motels, and putting them through the rigors of a sporting circuit, minus the glamour.

Working with Ivan as a therapist was always a pleasure because he was such a perfectionist and so dedicated. He grew to know his body very well and was always generous with his advice with young players coming onto the tour about how to look after themselves. I used to have regular sessions with him away from the tour in the days when he was training for the Australian Open which, in the early eighties, was still played on grass at Kooyong. He would come down to the Gleneagles Country Club in Florida, not far from Coral Springs where I was living at the time, and I would drive over to put the finishing touches to his training which usually involved maintenance work – deep tissue therapy to ease the stiffness in shoulder or lower back. He had Roche with him at the time and Tony was perfect for him as a coach, a serious tennis expert working with a very serious player. He used to bring Bill Scanlon in from Texas as a practice partner and they would all go over to Palm Beach to play on Jack Nicklaus' grass court. Nicklaus has always been a huge tennis fan and was introduced to Lendl by the IMG agent Bud Stanner who looked after both of them. For once, I don't think there was any financial arrangement involved. I think the deal was straightforward. Lendl and Scanlon could use the court as long as Jack and his wife Barbara got to play a little doubles with them afterwards!

I always feel Lendl, partially because of his lack of rapport with the public and to a lesser, extent the media, has never been given his due when people speak of the greatest players of all time. He racked up an incredible record, winning a total of 94 titles; eight of which were Grand Slams earned from an amazing nineteen finals. Only Wimbledon, where he reached the final twice, eluded him. Like so many Czechs, if you look up their records, Ivan was a slow starter at the highest level. Although he burst onto the scene in 1980 with seven ATP titles in what was only his second full year on the tour, it was not until 1984, when he was 24, that he actually won his first Slam title – in the infamous match against John McEnroe at Roland Garros when the American had led by two sets to love.

They were a funny pair, Lendl and McEnroe, and I don't mean in a jokey way. There were moments during their careers when they really hated each other although I am sure an uneasy calm has settled over their relationship now that they are both appearing on the ATP Champions tour. Their antipathy derived from the fact that they were such completely different people and viewed each other with complete incomprehension. "How could he be like that?" You could put the quote in both of their mouths. At one time or another they both uttered it.

By 1994, Lendl's back was giving him so many problems that he brought his remarkable career to an end. As we have seen, he never saved himself from the wear and tear of an incredibly stressful physical existence. The lower back area took more and more of the strain and generally, the aches and pains just kept on getting worse. Fifteen years is longer than most top players survive on the tour because, unlike the middle ranked guys who tend to play no more than two or three matches in an average week, the champions who are getting through to finals are playing five or six. The difference in work load is considerable and Lendl's career took him into the beginning of the modern era that has seen an enormous uptick in the sport's physicality. Ivan was not about to complain about that. How could he? Tennis as a physical sport had Lendl's name written all over it.

Recently, of course, Andy Murray has had first- hand proof of that, having been clever enough to hire Lendl as his coach. It was a somewhat daring move because Ivan had never coached a top player before but the chemistry worked, not least because Murray found himself able to enjoy the special Lendl humor. Relentless hard work was at the root of their successful relationship and of course, the young Scot thrived with his new mentor, winning a Gold Medal at Wimbledon in the 2012 Olympics before going to claim his first Grand Slam at the US Open. Then he capped it all with his 2013 Wimbledon triumph. Britain had waited 77 years for that priceless moment and I am sure Ivan felt a special pride in having helped Andy achieve it.

It was typical, I felt, that Lendl decided he could not offer Murray enough time to work with him properly when Andy returned to the tour following his back surgery in the fall of 2013. He had been hired to turn the talended Scot into a Grand Slam winner and in Ivan's mind, I suspect he felt that was mission accomplished. He is, and always was, his own man.

Chapter 10: Becker and Edberg

It was Wimbledon 1985 and I was having a routine sort of day in the No 1 locker room at the All England Club, giving some treatments for players coming off court, taping some feet for players preparing to play. Then I got the call that played a part in changing Wimbledon history. Boris Becker, the 17-year-old German kid everyone was talking about that year, had called for the athletic trainer out on Court 14.

The call had come through from the referee's office which is always in touch with all chair umpires by direct phone. Immediately alarm bells went off in my head because this was the young man who had badly damaged an ankle on Court One while trailing the talented Texan, Bill Scanlon, by two sets to one the year before. It hadn't been the happiest of debuts in the main draw at Wimbledon for this strapping teenager with the flame colored hair. He was forced to default and spent several weeks in rehab.

So I picked up my bag and rushed out in the direction of Court 14, bumping into Alan Mills, the referee, coming out of his office as I did so. Together we pushed our way through the dense crowds on the concourse – the usual Wimbledon mixture of smartly attired ladies in hats and young men on their second or third beer of the afternoon. It took a little while and my co-author Richard Evans, who had been witnessing the drama unfold while commentating for BBC Radio, tells me it seemed like ages before I eventually scrambled over the rope and got to Becker's side.

Although I didn't know it at the time, Becker had come within a nano second of de-faulting the match to Tim Mayotte, a fine American grass court player who had reached the Wimbledon semi-final three years previously. Becker had seemingly turned an ankle as he lunged for a ball in his typically all-or-nothing style and obviously fearing the worst after his experience of the year before, started limping towards the net with his hand held out – ready to default the match to

Mayotte. Almost simultaneously, Becker's manager, Ion Tiriac, and his coach, Gunther Bosch, hissed, "Wait! Call for the athletic trainer!" Boris stopped dead in his tracks, lowered the arm that was only a few feet from Mayotte, and turned towards his chair.

You can never rush on court to help a player with pre-conceived ideas, especially when you haven't seen the actual moment of injury. But I knew the history of the ankle because I had treated him the year before and needed to find out quickly just how much more damage had been done. There was only minimal soft tissue swelling which was a good sign so then I started maneuvering the ankle laterally and then up and down by pushing up from underneath the toes – all the while looking straight into Becker's glacial blue eyes to gauge his reaction. He had full range of motion on the ankle and my immediate thought was that he was not feeling any great pain and that he would be able to continue. Nothing is ever certain in life but this is the sort of decision you can only come to by virtue of experience. Despite the hubbub going on around you and the enormity of the moment – this was a match that would send someone into the quarter finals at Wimbledon – you have to concentrate on this player and this ankle, computing the history; the tolerance for injury and the temperament you are dealing with. Already I had been impressed by Boris. For a 17-year-old he was very astute and knew his body well. He had worked hard to overcome the previous injury and after the initial moment of panic had died down, he responded to my more detached and rational assessment.

Of course, any decision I made would impact his opponent. I could have told Boris it would be dangerous for him to continue and that would have handed the match to Mayotte – a terrific guy and an American. I am an American. Did I ever let those thoughts trickle into my subconscious? Never in a million years. If I did, I could never have done the job.

As it was, I just made sure that the ankle passed the test for stability; sprayed it with a little ethyl chloride (a topical cold spray), taped the ankle and told him he could get back on court. The long delay had not been easy on Mayotte and with the crowd yelling for the plucky kid, Tim struggled to impose his own serve and volley game on the match as Boris started throwing himself about court again with all the wild abandon of youth and won 6-3, 4-6, 6-7, 7-6, 6-2.

As soon as I got Becker back in the locker room, Tiriac and Bosch were there in close attendance. "How is he doing?" asked Tiriac, "Will he be at risk if he plays his next match?" They were logical questions and I was happy to give my honest answers. It is always easier to deal with a player's manager or agent if that person has been a player himself and Tiriac had certainly been a player. The Romanian with the droopy moustache still, to this day, stands at No 11 on the all- time list for total victories in Davis Cup play with a win-loss record of 70-39. This was impressive. But the man's personality is even more so. By his very appearance he has been known to scare the daylights out of some people but he is professional to his finger tips and we had established a working relationship long before, when he was still wielding a racket on the tour. Bosch, a less dominating character, also of Romanian origin, had actually brought the boy Becker to Tiriac's attention when Boris was very young and proceeded to coach him through the early part of his career. So both these guys knew the score and were happy to take medical advice from someone they respected.

So, we worked on him for two hours with electrical therapy and icing and kept the ankle compressed to stop any swelling. He felt a little bit of discomfort in the following matches but nothing serious enough to prevent this remarkable young man from becoming the youngest male ever to win Wimbledon.

Like many people, I believe Becker's greatest achievement was returning to Wimbledon the following year and retaining his crown. The second time around he had to play with all the pressure of expectation. In 1985 he just went out there swinging and despite being far from stupid, never really quite understood what he was achieving. But you can't take it away from him. For the record, Becker beat the experienced Hank Pfister in four sets in the first round; took out another American, Matt Anger, in three easy sets in the second; came through a titanic battle with the No 7 seed from Sweden, Joakim Nystrom 9-7 in the fifth and then, after beating Mayotte, took care of the mercurial Frenchman Henri Leconte in four. That put him in the semis where he removed another seeded Swede, Anders Jarryd after losing the first set before going out on finals day to defeat Kevin Curren, the South African whose serve had helped destroy both John McEnroe and Stefan Edberg in straight sets in previous rounds, by a score of 6-3, 6-7, 7-6, 6-4. History was made. Good thing I got it right about the ankle!

I had to make the decision about Becker at a big moment in a big tournament but the status, venue or ranking of the players involved really doesn't matter. As the care giver on the tour it was my job to look after everyone equally, no matter if they were earning five million dollars a year or struggling to pay their hotel bill. And sometimes very serious medical decisions had to be made in unlikely places. But, obviously, this incident had a major bearing on the career of someone who would rapidly develop into one of the icons of the game and become a national hero in his own country. The extent to which he had caught the imagination of the German public became clear to me in a touching way when the US played Germany in Hamburg in the Davis Cup later that year. Even though I was working for the opposing team, Dr. Stauder, the President of the German Federation at the time, gave me an award during a ceremony at the Atlantic Hotel for having helped Becker win Wimbledon. It was a nice gesture.

But, as I said, not all the crucial decisions I have had to make have come at Grand Slam events. In 1975, we were at the Capitol Center in Largo, Maryland where Donald Dell ran a winter WCT tournament at the time as well as the Citi Championships which is still up and running in Washington in the summer. Jeff Simpson, a New Zealand Davis Cup player of that era, was playing a doubles match in partnership with Mike Estep, the little Texan who went to coach Martina Navratilova so successfully at the height of her career. Simpson and Estep were playing a qualifier called Gene Russo and a partner whose name I have forgotten in an early round match. Suddenly Russo unloaded a huge forehand straight at Simpson at the net and caught Jeff flush in the neck. The impact floored him. He was convulsing by the time I got to him and was trying to swallow his tongue. So I grabbed an instrument I did not have to use too often during my career, thank heaven, and pried his clenched teeth open with an oral plastic screw and then got hold of his tongue with a tongue forcep, specifically designed for such occasions. Meanwhile a colleague from the tournament staff was rubbing his neck and as soon as I had his tongue sorted out, he recovered quickly. He had been conscious all along and his eyes were not dilated. So I took a while to ice the area that had been struck, making the most of the fact that there was no limitation on injury time outs in those days. It was up to me to tell the umpire when I felt a player was fit to continue. Simpson made a quick recovery and I decided to let him play on – something I would not have done, even in those far off days, if he had been knocked unconscious. Recently a lot more research has gone into the after effects of concussion, which sets in, to varying degrees, as soon as you lose consciousness as a result of a blow and the whole thing is being taken much more seriously.

The incident has stuck in my mind because it was an unusual sort of injury. Not many players get hit in the neck! But it illustrated how, in my job, you needed to be ready for just about any eventuality.

Returning to the late eighties and early nineties, Becker and Stefan Edberg, two of the most dominant players of that period, suffered from more conventional ailments that were strictly aligned to their body type and styles of play. Becker was a heavy man with a low center of gravity and unbelievable strength in his legs. I was always treating him for the scratches and abrasions he would receive on his rapidly scarring knees – the inevitable result of diving about on concrete and clay and on his favorite surface, grass.

Edberg was all about quiet elegance. He had tall, angular features and was a beautiful athlete but his corkscrew service motion ensured that he suffered from lower back problems early in his career. Back in the sixties, Charlie Pasarell who was ranked No 1 in America before turning himself into a great tournament impresario at Indian Wells, suffered in just the same way because of the extreme twist and arching of his back as he began his service motion. Whereas Becker was more openly emotional, waters ran deep with Edberg and he would tend to get a little melancholy in a Swedish sort of way when his fitness bothered him. I remember needing to talk him through it during a treatment at the Stockholm Open one year. Like Becker, Stefan was a hard worker – as he had to be as long as he continued to have the upbeat Englishman Tony Pickard as his coach which, of course, he did. The two were inseparable through most of Edberg's career – two totally contrasting personalities who became fast friends.

Both Becker and Edberg were mentally strong. I think most people would expect Boris to be the tougher personality but Stefan was often underestimated on that score because of his easy charm and sweet demeanor. But it took enormous mental resolve for Edberg to win back to back US Opens in a city whose brash life style did not fit easily with his personality. And although Becker finished with a decisive winning record against him in all matches, Edberg was not cowed by the big occasion and ended up winning two of the three consecutive Wimbledon finals they played against each other between 1988 and 1990.

Chapter 11: Celebrities

It is natural, I suppose, given my line of work that when you meet someone, it doesn't take long for them to start talking about their aches and pains. This is true, not only of a jogger or club tennis player but also of Princes, Princesses and Presidents. It also applies to the entertainers I have treated and advised on their various tennis injuries.

The first time I went to the White House was with a group of NBA players in 1963. It was about two months before President Kennedy was shot. He came to talk to the group and mingle a little with the players and on hearing that I was the athletic trainer, soon started talking about his chronic back problems which forced him to have a spinal fusion. He told me about the braces he had to wear around his lower back. In those days, before they started using neoprene, the brace was strengthened by little metal staves. Not too comfortable, I imagined. But he did speak fondly of his rocking chair which helped ease the stiffness and nothing has changed in that respect. Anyone with back problems would do well to invest in a rocking chair.

It has been my good fortune to be invited to the White House several times on various sporting occasions but the most memorable was in 1982 when President Reagan decided to honor the US Ski team and the Davis Cup squad that had just participated in an epic victory over Sweden in St Louis – the tie that saw John McEnroe win one of the longest matches in history, over six hours, against Mats Wilander.

Once again, the President of the time discovered what I did and suddenly I found myself in the role of advisor to the man himself.

President Reagan was not a young man by then and the back problems he had inherited from an active sporting career in his youth – he had played a lot of football – were acting up to the extent that he suffered from attacks of sciatica with the pain running right down his leg.

I made some suggestions as to the management of his current condition and he seemed to have a clearer understanding of what I proposed to him. President Reagan was just like his public image – amiable, chatty and relaxed.

Royals are a different breed, primarily, I suppose, because they have no need to win your vote! While some seem to have earned a reputation for being "more or less aloof" to pinch a line from that song in "High Society", that was certainly not the case with Princess Grace or Princess Diana.

I met Princess Diana by chance at the Vanderbilt Club, an indoor private members club near Shepherds Bush in London which has now been demolished. It was an extension of the club that used to exist at Grand Central Station in New York and became the gathering place for London's tennis-playing smart set. A WCT World Doubles Championship was held at the nearby Olympia complex one year and the ever-welcoming Charles Swallow, who ran the Vanderbilt, offered practice time to some of the pros.

I was over there tending to a few of the guys when I suddenly found myself being introduced to this stunning looking woman, all decked out in her tennis gear. Princess Diana was not only a real tennis fan and follower of the pro tour but she liked to play as much as possible, mostly with a group of girl friends.

As a result of seeing me running around at the Queen's Club during the Stella Artois Championships which she attended regularly, she seemed to know who I was and it didn't take long for her to say, "Mr. Norris, I have a problem!"

It was not a very unusual one – a form of tennis elbow that flares up on the outside of the elbow as a result of hitting the ball late. If you do this on a regular basis – as many amateur players do – the extensor muscles in the forearm get inflamed and feed pain back up into the elbow. She was already wearing an arm brace but evidently felt she needed some advice of how to manage her elbow. I was able to put her in the right direction with the correct counseling.

It was all a bit surreal but you could not feel uncomfortable for long in Princess Diana's presence. She was a charming and extremely gregarious person who quickly began chatting away about the tour and revealing how keenly she followed it.

It must have been about three years later when I was in the training room at Flushing Meadows, just finishing off some treatment late one Saturday night when someone came in with the news of the car crash in Paris. I couldn't believe it. Having had the good fortune to meet her, the confirmation of her death the following day hit me all the harder. It was a shocking end to such a vibrant young life.

It is hard to rationalize how fate decreed that Europe's other much loved Princess should also lose her life in a car accident. As the world knows Princess Grace of Monaco was driving down the Corniche with her daughter Stephanie when she apparently lost control of the car on one of those hairpin bends and crashed. It was, of course, totally traumatic for Stephanie but many believe that Prince Rainier never really recovered from the loss.

The whole family was devastated and I grieved especially for Grace's brother, Jack Kelly, who I had gotten to know quite well over the years. Our friendship began way back during my days in the NBA when Tom Gola of the New York Knicks introduced us on a trip to Philadelphia. Kelly was, of course, a renowned oarsman but he loved to play tennis, too and was often down at the Le Club International in Fort Lauderdale in the winter months. When I switched over to tennis and became a regular visitor to Philadelphia to work at the WCT events run by that amazing entrepreneur Marilyn Fernberger, Jack and I used to have lunch together. So I had an easy introduction to the Grimaldi family during the Monte Carlo Open which was always one of the highlights of the European season.

Like the rest of her family, Princess Grace was a keen tennis player – it would have been silly not to have been, considering she had the splendid Monte Carlo Country Club, with its breathtaking views of the Mediterranean at her disposal! But, once again, it was that tennis elbow problem which started giving her pain so I was able to treat her for that as well as some back pain. Despite her years on the Cote d'Azur, Princess Grace came across as a thoroughly American lady, always outgoing and totally charming.

Prince Rainier was an avid player himself and his son, Prince Albert, who now rules over the Principality, quickly caught the bug and has always enjoyed hitting with the pros, so many of whom reside in Monaco and use the Country Club for their practice sessions. In recent years, Novak Djokovic has had the occasional hit with Prince Albert. That's one of the perks of running the place – you get to play with the best!

In 2000, we had the opportunity to be invited to Buckingham Palace for the Wimbledon re-match of Borg-McEnroe. It was held on the first Sunday of the fortnight. This match out in the Palace Gardens on their hard court was arranged by Prince Andrew. The attendees were there in support of his charity, Prevention of Cruelty to Children. I was there to provide medical coverage for the players, as I had so many years at Wimbledon. I was very touched, when introduced to the Prince, "Bill Norris needs no introduction; I have witnessed his magic treating the players on Centre Court so many times!"

In addition to royalty, I have treated many actors and singers like Dustin Hoffman, Diana Ross, Kenny Rogers and Barry Gordy of Motown fame. I remember one time in Los Angeles when Hoffman came to the tournament as Jimmy Connors' guest and asked if I could work on his back while Jimmy was getting treated. I put the muscle stimulator on him and kept increasing the intensity to a level that he could tolerate, all the while thinking of his scene in the dentists' chair being tortured by Laurence Olivier! I was a little gentler.

All these celebrities have a basic need: to be treated by someone that has treated the best athletes. Everyone feels if this man can make John McEnroe feel better, then maybe he can make me feel better too! Nowadays, I see this same attitude. My practice is based on the track record that I achieved the past fifty years. People will say "Bill, you really paid your dues and now you can relax." I say, "You never really finish paying your dues." Once you set the standard for excellence, you need to maintain that same standard.

Anything less than that is unacceptable. When I look at myself in the mirror, it makes me feel good to know that I made a difference.

Chapter 12: The Top Four

"Bill was always there for us with a smile and his positive attitude always gave me the necessary confidence to recover from injuries."

— Rafa Nadal

Throughout my years on the ATP Tour there were frequent periods when a couple of players ruled the roost and for a time in the mid-eighties, just after Bjorn Borg retired, the trio of John McEnroe, Ivan Lendl and Mats Wilander grabbed most of the major titles. But the game has never known an era in which four super stars turned the top of the men's game into a little private club with a big sign on the door of Grand Slam finals that said, "No Admittance!"

From 2005 to 2013 only two players – Marat Safin in '05 at the Australian Open and Juan Martin Del Potro at the 2009 US Open – were able to tear that sign off the door and win a Slam. Of the 36 Grand Slams played during that period 34 were won by either Roger Federer, Rafael Nadal, Novak Djokovic or Andy Murray. Amazing.

Federer has always been the leader of the pack, on court and off. Although Nadal is still out there chasing, Federer's record of 17 Grand Slam singles titles may well stand forever and you can guarantee that no one will match his astonishing achievement of reaching the semi-final or better in 23 CONSECUTIVE Slams. Given the beating the body takes as a result of the ever increasing physicality of the sport, it is difficult for most players to survive uninjured that long, let alone play well enough to reach the semi-final each and every time.

Federer has managed it because he puts less pressure on his body than most players. He is a light runner as opposed to someone like Nadal who is a heavy runner. Roger skims the surface with those dancing feet which, when he is on song, always get him to the ball at precisely the right moment. Not surprisingly he went through a difficult period when he contracted a relatively light dose of mononucleosis in 2007 and he was not quite at his best as the new season started. The result was that he only got as far as the semis (only!) at the 2008 Australian Open and for the first time, we saw him shanking some balls. When that happens to a top player, look to the feet. A split second late to the ball and the timing is a split second off, causing havoc with the shot. If you are suffering from the after effects of a virus like mono, that is what can happen.

It didn't stop him reaching the final of Roland Garros and Wimbledon that year and bouncing back to win the US Open. His level of consistency over the years, even up to 2013 when his ranking started to drop, has been astonishing and it all comes back to the fact that his body type and style of play has enabled him to avoid serious injury. In that respect he reminds me of Jimmy Connors and Ken Rosewall. Both had pure strokes which virtually eliminated the jarring and twisting of ligaments that occurs when players adopt extreme grips to impart huge amounts of top spin. Rosewall, whose career stretched well into his forties, had very little understanding of what it meant to be injured and in fact, the only time he asked me for anything more than rubdown was when he hurt his neck gardening!

Federer has been playing in a different era and even he would not have survived in the lightweight plimsolls that Kenny and most of his colleagues in the 50's and 60's used to wear. We used to pad Roger's feet with foam rubber and bandage the bottoms of his feet. He had a weak ankle early on and that needed a careful strapping job before every match. We worked on his core, too, which was where he tended to get tight but he was always very responsive to advice and always had a great attitude.

I had first known his mother, Lynette Federer, when she was working in the credentials office at the St Jacobs Halle in Basle – the home of the Swiss Indoors, an event tournament director Roger Brennwald had started in the mid seventies. The little kid hitting balls on some of the outdoor courts while mom was working was also named Roger. Brennwald has been laughing about it ever since. "Here I was paying fortunes to get the best players in the world to come to my tournament not realizing we were growing the best player ever right here in our back yard," he used to tell us.

It is the mark of how he was brought up that Roger is gracious and unfailingly polite to everyone he meets. I remember an occasion when he shared a courtesy car with Sherie and our daughter Lisa to Roland Garros one year at the start of the tournament. When they arrived, Sherie, who does not speak French, began having a tough time gaining entrance to the accreditation office. Without prompting, Roger, who didn't know my family at all at the time, stepped in and smoothed their passage. In England, I think they would call him 'A proper gent.'

Nadal looked like a kid who wanted to learn from the moment that he first appeared on the tour at sixteen. You could tell he was inquisitive and apart from the ever present Uncle Toni, who had started coaching him at the age of four, he learned a lot from his fellow Mallorcan Carlos Moya. We watched him grow from a skinny kid into this heavily muscled athlete and the first problem I had to deal with concerning Rafa was an ankle sprain. It was his left ankle and I think that injury ultimately started to affect his left knee. He had struggled a little with his right knee, too, from time to time but it was always his patella tendon on his left knee that needed extra support with some tape just below the knee cap. Ankle problems can move up the leg and start affecting the knee, one of the most complicated joints in the human body. The problem has, of course, plagued his career but that has not stopped him from becoming one of the greatest winners of all time. His come back in 2013, regaining the world No 1 ranking after spending most of the previous year sidelined because of his knees, was a staggering achievement.

Nadal certainly had major problems with his knees but, sadly, he has not been the only one. The Yugoslav, Goran Prpic, played most of his career with a huge Lennox Hill brace (named after the New York hospital) to support a chronically damaged knee. Peter McNamara's career was virtually ruined when he twisted his knee after tripping on an irregular piece of court in Rotterdam and one just holds one's breath whenever the incredibly athletic Frenchman Gael Monfils throws himself about the court. Monfils has suffered from all manner of injuries to his knees, ankles and shoulder and we have tried to do our best for him but it is a challenge! Gael, with his Caribbean heritage, is a dynamic personality who attracts fans all over the world and one just hopes he can stay fit long enough to do justice to his great talent. He is certainly one of the best athletes ever to play the game.

The same can be said of Rafa who may look fierce on court but he is one of the nicest, most polite young men you could ever wish to meet. He is also quiet generous, too, and has helped more friends and charities financially than one would ever know. He's a gem.

I am also a huge admirer of Djokovic. Like Nadal, Novak is always wanting to learn and will talk to anyone, including lower ranked players in an attempt to swap experiences and glean little bits of information. Even a player ranked 200 might have had a brush with greatness, a little moment that might open the jar of knowledge and Djokovic is the type of guy who feasts off every tidbit.

I first came across him when he was practicing with Ivan Ljubicic and Ljubi's long time coach Ricardo Piatti at the Monte Carlo Country Club. He was still very young then and was obviously a guy who liked to enjoy himself. He started showing off on court with his impersonations of John McEnroe, Maria Sharapova and other players and they were hilarious. But he quickly sensed that some members of the locker room resented it and offering the first evidence of his keen intelligence, he dropped the act. Like many youngsters, he was learning how to balance professionalism with some foolishness and he cottoned on to what was acceptable quicker than most. Almost always, look at a champion and you are looking at a fast learner.

Djokovic certainly looked like a champion in the making and he became a big one in 2008 when he won the Australian Open. However, there were doubts about his physical abilities at that stage because he frequently suffered breathing problems, especially in extreme heat. Early on in his career I had been summoned to an outside court at Flushing Meadows to try and alleviate a problem Novak was having with his breathing on a hot and humid day at the US Open. It can be a panicky situation for a player and the first thing you need to offer is reassurance, along with ways to lower the body temperature with ice packs.

Not surprisingly, Novak sought out the best doctors he could find and he was taught breathing techniques which helped the problem along with a much-publicized switch to gluten-free diet. Once this change started to kick in, the package was complete because Djokovic has that tall, lean frame which is ideal for a tennis player. He is not overly muscular but, as we have seen in the numerous marathon matches he has become involved in with other members of the Top 4, he has proved himself to be very durable now that the fear of not being able to breath freely is no longer a factor.

The manner in which he started to dominate the game in 2011, kicking off with another Australian Open title and a stunning streak of 41 consecutive matches unbeaten (Federer eventually broke the run at Roland Garros) was quite incredible. Proving what a complete player he had become, he went on to fulfill a boyhood dream and win Wimbledon that year. Needless to say he rose to No 1 in the world and on and off the court, became the greatest ambassador Serbia could have had. He has drawn a close knit team around him, headed by his Slovak coach Marion Vajda, to whom he has remained loyal through thick and thin, even since bringing Boris Becker into the mix. Novak has developed into a very impressive personality. He takes his responsibilities to his country and the game he plays so well, very seriously. I have always enjoyed watching these young men develop from adolescence into mature human beings and given the pressures he is always under from a nation thirsting for success, few have impressed me more.

When I first met Andy Murray around 2002 he was a shy boy with a long, stringy body and an interesting game. It would have taken a big leap of faith to predict that he would turn into a powerful, muscular athlete with sufficient talent and willpower to satisfy a nation's craving and win Wimbledon. When he did, finally, become the first British male to claim the world's most prestigious title since 1936 in 2013, it seemed clear to me that Andy's primary emotion as he laid his hands on that beautiful gold trophy was one of relief.

Djokovic, his opponent in the final, knows a thing or two about a nation's expectations and he quickly acknowledged that no one had been under greater pressure to perform that day than Murray. A year earlier the tall Scot had lost to Federer in the final but since then he had won the Olympic gold medal on that same Centre Court and cracked his Grand Slam hoodoo by winning the US Open in his fifth Slam final. So there was no longer any doubt that Murray COULD win Wimbledon. But WOULD he? A nation held its breath as he stepped up to serve for the match and practically passed out en masse when he missed two match points and allowed Djokovic a break back point. Afterwards many critics said that they felt Murray would have lost the match had he lost that point because Novak is very capable of turning a duel inside out. Murray held it together, winning the next three points and so becoming the first Brit since Fred Perry seventy seven years before to keep the title in Britain. Knowing Fred as I did, I think he would have been genuinely pleased for the young man while gritting his teeth a little at no longer being remembered as "the last man to........" All champions have an ego and Perry had a big one.

In the early years, Murray was not a frequent visitor to my treatment room but I was needed in a hurry when he slipped on the Centre Court at the Queen's Club in 2005 and sprained his ankle. We strapped him up and I used my electrical equipment and ice packs after the match to keep the swelling down. The British media went into a tizzy about Andy's chances of playing in what was destined to be his first Wimbledon but there was never much danger of his pulling out. The ankle was damaged but not severely and the kid was running on adrenaline. He went on to reach the third round at Wimbledon and set in motion one of the great success stories of British tennis. In fact, given the company he is keeping in this demanding era of the game, it is hard to argue against Murray being the greatest British tennis player of all time.

The injury was a warning sign and Murray quickly took the precaution of protecting the ankle with a brace that he still wears to this day. These things eventually become psychological and he would probably feel naked without it. The work that his two fitness trainers, Jez Green and Matt Little, have put Andy through over the past several years has turned him into a formidable athlete. He has more muscle density than Djokovic and until he needed back surgery after the 2013 US Open, he was capable of withstanding those marathon matches the top guys put themselves through nowadays as well as anyone.

Andy has always been a very amenable and approachable guy to have around but it helps if you understand his very dry Scottish sense of humor. I like to pride myself as being pretty with it on the humor front but you have to be quick with Andy. I think one of the reasons Lendl proved to be such a vital addition to Team Murray is that they enjoyed each other's sense of humor. Luckily Jez and the guys seemed to be able to roll with the punches in the pranks department. So, too, does Amelie Mauresmo who, to the surprise of some, was Murray's choice as coach to replace Lendl. She will bring something different to the group, of course, but early evidence suggests she is fitting in well.

Chapter 13: The Doctors

"As one of the Medical Directors I have seen Bill in an even different light not only that wonderful physiotherapist, mentor and player confidant but a true ambassador of our sport. I have turned to him many times for his wise counsel and good judgment. It has been a rare privilege to have served with him all these years and I am fortunate enough to call him a very close friend."

— David Dines, M.D.

As I reflect on my career as a sports medicine therapist in professional tennis, one of the things that makes me happiest is the way the medical practitioners involved in tennis have come together to provide better coverage at tournaments worldwide.

When I started on the Tour there were times that the sports medicine therapist was the only constant. I have been at tournaments when I was the only caregiver present.

As time went by, tournaments were enlisting the aid of volunteer physicians. Meanwhile, the Tour gave me some assistance by employing additional sports medicine therapists. I was covering forty weeks of tournaments at that time. By getting an extra set of hands, I could reduce my workload. At tournaments we would develop local teams of physiotherapists, athletic trainers and massage therapists. The development of these teams still exists and has proven to be a valuable asset. Because professional tennis is played on several continents, there are times that three tournaments are played during the week around the world.

The first few years were real eye openers in a sense. We did have physicians volunteering to help with the coverage, usually because they were tennis fans. But, unfortunately, that did not mean they had the faintest idea of how to handle tennis related injuries! They certainly did not know about the specific problems created overhead, by which I mean stresses and strains created from the repetitive motions required while serving or hitting an overhead.

Tennis medical coverage has been for the most part, volunteer-based. In Europe, some physicians are paid something, not too much, but enough to cover some of their expenses. In the rest of the world, physicians volunteer their time to cover the medical needs of the players, officials and spectators.

In the early years, I remember one time in Philadelphia when the volunteer physician turned out to be a gynecologist. Here we have a men's tournament and the physician's area of expertise is not exactly what the players are likely to need! Whoever at the tournament accepted his willingness to help, did not check out his qualifications!

After a few of these mess-ups, I drafted up some criteria for what help we needed to adequately cover a world-class tennis event. In most cases, the tournament was relieved to know they had someone to help with the selection process of having the appropriate physicians and massage therapists.

In the U.S., we have always thought of the lead physician to be an orthopaedist. In the rest of the world, the sports doctor usually is a physician that has a working knowledge of orthopaedics, family practice medicine and general medicine. His training can be family practice sports medicine. In some U.S. tournaments we would have an orthopaedist as well as a family practice physician.

We found that this system was most effective when we had communication with the medical team throughout the year. In planning medical coverage for a tournament, the reality is that no one physician can cover the tournament by himself. He has his own practice to look out for and that is the way it should be. We need the tournament physician to have other doctors' help with the coverage. The lead tournament physician is responsible for making the medical coverage schedule. The ideal situation is where there is an orthopaedist and a family practice physician on site for the day session. These two physicians are relieved by two others that will come and cover the night session. The day session physicians will inform the night session physicians of what went on, what they had to deal with and give them an update to insure continuity of care.

There are some disciplines of tennis heath care that do not have to be on site at the tournament. Caregivers such as dentists, chiropractors, podiatrists, cardiologists, internists, etc. should be on call and available but not on site.

An integral component of the tournament is to have emergency medical technicians on site to administer emergency care to everyone involved. There have been cases at tournaments where a tennis player needed transport to the hospital. Many times when a player suffered from heat illness, the EMTs were available to treat them on site with intravenous hydration. Spectators are always the target at tournaments when there are heat issues. It is wise to have the emergency medical technicians on site from the time that the gates are open to the public to the closing down of each day's activity.

Massage therapy has been a much utilized modality for the players. Each player benefits from having massage. These therapists work long hours and are appreciated by the players. They are an important component of the medical team.

I was happy to be able to help coordinate the original Physicians Conference that was held at the ATP's headquarters in Ponte Vedra, Florida and later in London, Lisbon and other venues. We invited a wide range of doctors who had been involved in the tour like David Dines from the US Open, US Davis Cup team doctor and the Hamlet Cup on Long Island, David Altchek, US Davis Cup team doctor; Hartmut Krahl from Essen, Germany; Gary Windler from Charleston, South Carolina and Per Renstrom of Sweden. They presented research papers; discussed the various problems they had faced while treating players on the tour and generally helped to unify this far-flung operation.

You never know what crisis is going to blow up and sometimes it really does come out of left field. When Thomas Muster was hit by a car in Miami on the eve of the '89 Lipton final, I was taking the evening off and was relieved that my highly efficient colleague Todd Snyder was on duty to handle the ramifications which, of course, included getting Thomas into the hospital. The Miami doctor Charles Virgin was pro-active in opening up a dialogue with Muster's doctor in Vienna so that we could get him flown home as soon as possible.

Communication skills are vital for an ATP Sports Medicine Therapist who acts as the orchestrator of the tournament medical services team. It is his responsibility to coordinate the interaction of each member of the team and he should be in contact with the physicians, massage therapists, emergency medical technicians, the ATP Supervisor and tournament directors.

The ATP Medical Services Department is responsible for the management of player's medical records. The Tour developed its own medical data recording system that has been most helpful in addressing the players' medical needs. Tennis medicine research continues as a result of this data that has been collected and the information is always available to the tournament physician who will pass details of what has taken place to his counterpart at the next event so as to ensure continuity of player care.

It's a big, fascinating, diverse world out there and modern technology has, happily, made it a far more coordinated one. For me, it's been a privilege to have been part of it, helping to alleviate the pain and hopefully, dilute the stress with a few laughs. Tennis players are an amazing bunch of athletes, probably more resilient, dedicated and strong in both body and mind than some observers can comprehend. Like our great game, they are just getting stronger.

Chapter 14: A Different Life

After all those decades on the road, with my devoted wife Sherie by my side, our life is very different now. We are at home in Boca Raton, in a house we have lived in for 20 years and everyone comes to me. What a change.

Chris Evert always said that when I left the tour, I could look after the kids at her place across the road and that is what I am doing. Out of the thirty patients I see a week, some are junior players from the Evert Academy and the Rick Macci Academy. Some are local, and mostly aging, players from the area who need patching up so that they can stay on court. Tennis is their life and most are prepared to suffer a little pain to keep hitting balls. For them it really is pain, set and match!

Sometimes I end up looking after an entire family. Steven and Pnina Milstein are a case in point. It began with treating their daughter, Adi when she played at the Evert Academy. Her two brothers, Ben and Oren were next to need my help. Ben is a point guard in basketball and Oren is a kicker for his high school football team. One day Mom hobbled over, having sprained her ankle while Dad started to get problems from continuous running on the beach. If you do that you have to remember you are mostly running on a slope which means that one leg, in effect, becomes shorter than the other. That tends to put a lot of things further up the body out of whack!

I'm happy to take care of all the Milstein's various aches and pains and the need to look after all ages and both genders has certainly improved my knowledge and areas of expertise. This is true particularly in dealing with parents. One only came into direct professional contact with parents now and again on the ATP Tour but, of course, the young teenagers from Evert's are usually accompanied by mom or dad or both when they visit me.

I have mentioned the problems resulting from over-playing youngsters in previous chapters and it is something I am always monitoring. When I'm confronted with a parent and child, I make a point of directing my questions at the child. I want to look into their eyes and gauge their true feelings. If they are feeling a little beat up, is it just because of a teenage mood or is there some other reason? Are they hurting because of a real injury or the aches and pains that come naturally from a growth spurt? And the biggest question of all: Is this relentless commitment to tennis motivated by their own desires and aspirations or that of a parent?

These are not easy questions to answer, especially when you add in the education factor. Most of the kids I see are home-schooled or study online in the upstairs class room at Evert's. Some go to Boca Prep right across the street where Andy Roddick and Mardy Fish were once students. In those days, Andy used to love coming over for his favorite meal – one of Sherie's prime rib dinners. He was a lively, amusing youngster and there was never much doubt that he was dedicated to the idea of becoming a champion.

But it is all a big workload for someone going through those difficult formative years and parents need to be constantly reminded of the stress involved – both to themselves and their children. They need to rest occasionally so that body and mind can recharge the batteries.

While treating some of the young players from the Evert Academy over the past few years, I have been impressed by the professionalism and dedication of girls like Madison Keys, Lauren Davis and the Swiss youngster Belinda Bencic who are doing everything necessary to maximize their talents on the pro tour. They seem to have gotten the balance right between working really hard and knowing when to rest. But the very fact that teenagers have needed to come and see me with aches and pains resulting from growth spurts offers evidence of just how careful one has to be with young athletes. When I treated Madison and Belinda their growth plates were still open which means real injuries can be masked by this natural process.

In the meantime, I keep up to date with the latest medical and technical developments in the world of sports medicine.

Like everything else in our crazy cyber space age, advances and innovations come thick and fast and as a result, players are so much better off than they were when I first started in the business.

Now I am able to make use of the newest technology such as the therapeutic super pulsed low level laser. This modality addresses pain. This treatment provides patients with a safe, effective and painless therapy that uses the body's own natural healing systems to relieve pain, increase joint mobility, increase tissue integrity and promote cell regeneration.

The laser works by supplying energy to the body in the form of billions of photons of light. The body absorbs this laser light on a cellular level and transforms it to chemical energy, which the body then uses to commence its own tissue repairs. The bio-stimulating effect of laser therapy causes a decrease in inflammation and pain and an increase in tissue regeneration and healing.

Over two thousand clinical studies worldwide have proven the success of therapeutic lasers in the healing of neural muscular-skeletal conditions. Conditions such as low back pain, neck pain, arthritis, heel pain, tennis elbow, knee pain, tendinitis, sprains and strains, carpal tunnel syndrome, hip pain, wound healing and more are successfully treated with super pulsed low level laser.

Today, players, both amateur and professional, are much more aware of their bodies and how to take care of them. Preventative exercises, like going through a proper warm-up, are routine now, certainly for the pros but more and more for the occasional player as well.

And the pros, of course, live in a completely different world from the days when Fred Stolle had to ask my co-writer Richard Evans for an Alka-Seltzer so that he could focus properly on the Roland Garros doubles final after a long, champagne-filled night at the Lido!

Today's professionals have to be prepared mentally to deal with the intensity of the spotlight that is on them day and night, with the media scrutinizing their every act and utterance. They had less need of help in Stolle's day and in any case, there wasn't much of it until Donald Dell, the first real agent for tennis players, and then Mark McCormack came along.

For me personally, it's been a long and fascinating road and the rewards have come simply through the work that I love and interaction with such an amazing variety of personalities all over the world. But it is always nice to get recognized and I was thrilled to be the recipient of the International Tennis Hall of Fame's Tennis Educational Merit Award in March 2014. The award is presented to those who have made a notable contribution to tennis education at the national level and I felt honored to find myself amongst such great honorees as former Stanford University coach Dick Gould; Allen Fox, his counter part at Pepperdine and author of books on sports psychology; Arthur Ashe and another great educator, Peter Burwash.

The function was held at LaCosta, the resort near San Diego where Pancho Segura ran the tennis for so many years. Stan Smith, who is President of the International Tennis Hall of Fame, was MC for the ceremonies. I was presented by Todd Ellenbecker, who I mentored and was my logical choice to succeed me as Administrator of Medical Services at the ATP. It was an emotional moment for me as Todd recounted how he had first contacted "Mr. Norris" by writing a letter on a sheet of yellow legal paper to ask if he could observe how I worked when the tour came to Scottsdale, Arizona where he was living. I said yes and I remember putting him to work preparing ice packs for the players. He rose quickly as a sports physical therapist and it was heart warming to hear him say how much he and "many, many others in the medical industry" had benefited from my advice and guidance over the years.

So, in signing off the memory-lane part of this book, I want to say this: After all the time that I have devoted to helping others, I have lots of folks to thank. I have been blessed to have a wife and two children that have given me love and support throughout my career. Their love and support have fueled me to achieve so much. Sherie has always been there for me and thankfully, after forty-eight years, she continues to be by my side. My daughter Lisa has been my supporter and coach. She helped us so much on this book, spending hours and hours on this project to get it just right. We could not have done this without Lisa's help. Our son Darren and daughter-in-law, Ari, give me an objective perspective that is always helpful. They are always willing to go that extra mile for me. Ari did our cover for this book and helped with other parts of the book's interior. As you can see, it was a family affair. Last but not least, my parents Elizabeth and Lester taught me a good work ethic. I made sure to pass this on to my children. I want to thank all the photographers for their contributions. Thanks to Todd Ellenbecker for his shoulder expertise in the Pain section of the book, John Mark Jenkins for his help with all the exercises (he's my model in the photos), the ATP athletic trainers, the ATP tournament physicians, my Davis Cup captains, and finally my "players" who have been so great to work with all these years. You all make it fun.

Thank you for reading thus far. I hope the following pages will help you stay on court!

February 2, 1975, I took a picture with Borg and
Ashe before their WCT Richmond tournament
final. Borg won 4-6, 6-4, 6-4 in Arthur's
hometown. Photo: Bill Norris Collection

William Clyde Tulley was our WCT mascot and
his son was the LA Strings mascot. Photo: Kurt
Wallace

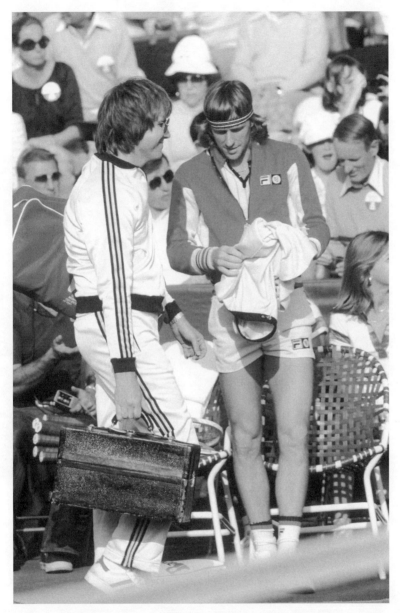

1977 US Open, Bjorn Borg needed my help.
Photo: Art Seitz

1978 World Team Tennis Champions Los
Angeles Strings. Front Row: Ann Kiyomura,
Chris Evert and Stephanie Tolleson. Back Row:
Bill Norris, Ashok Amritraj, Ilie Nastase and
Vijay Amritraj. Photo: Fred A. Sabine

1979 US Davis Cup World Champions celebrate after clinching title over Italy, December 15, 1979. Vitas Gerulaitis, Byron Radaker, Tony Trabert, Stan Smith, Bob Lutz, Bill Norris, Vitas Gerulaitis, Sr., Dr. Omar Fareed. Photo: Art Seitz

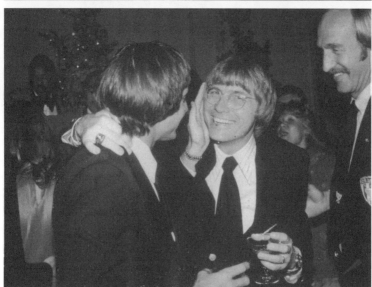

'79 US Davis Cup Bob, Stan and I celebrating
our win over Italy. Photo: Russ Adams

Arthur Ashe, Jr., US Davis Cup Captain, at
LaCosta Resort, Carlsbad, CA, March 1981.
Mexico vs US. Feeling hungry! Photo: Russ
Adams

Dr. Omar Fareed, US Davis Cup physician and tournament physician for the Pacific Southwest Championships. His proactive work prevented many illnesses to tennis players. Photo: Russ Adams

To Bill and Sheri Norris
With best wishes,
Ronald Reagan . Nancy Reagan

July 19, 1982, Sherie Norris and I met President
Ronald Reagan and First Lady Nancy Reagan at
the White House. Photo: White House Collection

Here's Jimmy Connors with my children, Lisa
and Darren taken at Columbus, Ohio, August
1982. Jimmy always had time for my family.
Photo: Tom Fey

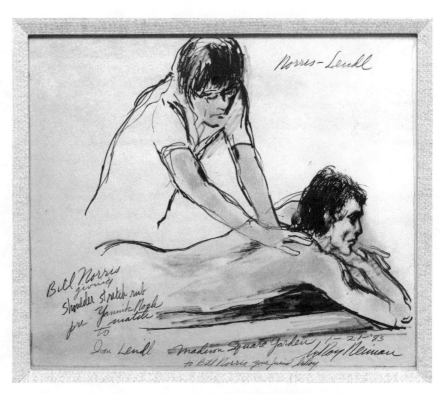

Norris-Lendl drawing by LeRoy Neiman prior to
Lendl-Yannick Noah 1982 Volvo Masters match.
January 21, 1983 at Madison Square Garden.

John McEnroe treated for wrist sprain at 1984
Davis Cup final in Gothenburg, Sweden, US vs
Sweden. Photo: Russ Adams

Seventeen year old Boris Becker sprains his left
ankle at the 1985 Wimbledon Championships. I
treated him and he returned to competition. He
went on to win the Championships becoming the
youngest man ever to win the title. Photo:
Michael Cole

Photo credit Russ Adams. April 7, 1988, Here,
I'm helping Andre tie his tie. 1988 Davis Cup 1st
round in Lima. USA won 3-0 over Peru. Photo:
Russ Adams

July 4, 1993, John McEnroe, Tim Gullikson and I
help Pete celebrate his first Wimbledon
Championship over Jim Courier 7-6, 7-6, 3-6, 6-3.
Photo: Bill Norris Collection.

Andre Agassi before his final 2006 US Open
match. It has been a long road traveled by both
since I first met him in Las Vegas when he was a
child. Photo: Bill Norris Collection

Mats Wilander, 2010 ATP Champions Event
Delray Beach, Fl. Photo: Bill Norris Collection

Kei Nishikori and I at the 2010 Delray ATP
tournament. Photo: Bill Norris Collection

John McEnroe at ATP Champions event, Delray
Beach, FL 2010. Photo: Bill Norris Collection

Andy Roddick and I, February, 2014 Delray
Beach. Photo: Bill Norris Collection

March 15, 2014 receiving International Tennis Hall of
Fame Tennis Educational Merit Award. Todd Ellenbecker was
my presenter. Photo: Susan and Fred Mullane

SECTION II:

The Pain Department

Chapter A: Knowing When to Stop in a Match

I look back to when I first started taking care of tennis players. Tennis players are usually hearty souls. They love the game and it is hard to get them to put the racquet down and rest even though there are injuries and overuse syndrome conditions that are very painful.

There are times that it becomes necessary to take oneself out of competition. Unfortunately, it's difficult for some people to acknowledge their vulnerability and a lot of tennis players think of themselves as being invincible.

I think this is the main message that I give to the tennis players: Would you rather play that one match that you have in your tank today or not be able to play for the next three weeks. We all have choices. It's how you make those choices. Be smart, it's your body!

Probably the most important rule in distinguishing between a pain that must be attended to and one that can be ignored is to know oneself. It's a learning process and the learning can't come from a book.

Still there are several hard and fast signs that tell you to stop:

Dizziness: pressure on the chest and or pain radiating down the arms, perhaps accompanied by shortness of breath, weakness and a sense of impending doom. It may not be a heart attack but do you want to take any chances?

Pain: that is severe enough for you not to be able to run side to side and to the net is a good indicator that you need to seek professional help.

Tingling: or numbness in the legs or pain radiating from the butt to the calf and in to the foot if you have been diagnosed with sciatica. The odds of having your 1st attack of sciatica during a match are very slight but if you know you have it and you develop these symptoms you run the risk of herniating a disc.

Chills: and the absence of perspiration on a hot day. Hyperthermia can occur even in a match that is not long in duration. If hyperthermia is not treated it has a high fatality rate. The problem is that many people are not aware that they are coming down with hyperthermia and may be confused and combative.

Exhaustion: and trouble staying on your feet can be due to any number of things including hyperthermia, and muscle problems. Your body is telling you to stop playing and get medical care.

As much as the ATP medical staff educates the players on the prevention of heat illness, there are some players that do not pay attention to what we are saying. Those are the ones that have to pay the price.

There are other signs that you need to take notice of before you continue playing:

A pain in the front of the hip or groin could be a stress fracture as could any pain that persists after running around on the court. If you have pain while walking you need medical attention. There have been cases where stress fractures have developed into displaced fractures where the ends of the bones separate. You need to address these problems immediately as some displaced fractures require surgery.

There is no point to punishing yourself with severe pain by staying on the court. In the long run, you are not helping yourself or your doubles partner. Tennis injuries and overuse syndrome conditions do happen. Don't think that you are so invincible that they can not happen to you. You need to remember that tennis takes no off season. Here in Boca Raton we have tournaments every week. You just have to use that noggin of yours and make the right choices with your health.

Chapter B: Preparation and Prevention

The more time you spend on a tennis court, or indulge in any energetic physical activity, the more various parts of your body are going to start crying "Help!" Muscles, ligaments, joints and even bones are going to start complaining. My job has been to address those complaints and I want to pass on to you what I have learned from tending to all manner of athletes from John McEnroe and Roger Federer to Doug Edwards, a 60-year-old who lives near me in Boca Raton, Florida and wants to spend every available moment of his life on a tennis court. Doug needs patching up from time to time. He is my poster boy for all those dedicated, if not downright fanatical, tennis players out there who refuse to allow the passing years to erode their enthusiasm for a sport that keeps them young.

Sooner or later – and sooner if you play on hard courts – everyone who plays tennis consistently is going to develop some kind of physical problem. The problem can be minimized with proper treatment but the best way to handle the whole issue is through Preparation and Prevention. So listen up and learn something!

Preparation

This does not start on the day of your match but the night before. Some will say days before that big match, that you need to prepare. Be careful of what you eat and be sure you drink plenty of fluids. The body needs time to absorb what you put into it and chugging a pint of water half an hour before you go on court is not going to do it.

So pick from the following:

Drinks: Water, fruit juice, vegetable juice and sports drinks that contain trace minerals (sodium, potassium, calcium, magnesium, etc.).

Fruits: Eat fruits such as all melon, cantaloupe, pineapple, peaches, and blueberries in small amounts.

Vegetables: Eat vegetables that are water based such as lettuce, carrots, celery, potatoes, jicama, radishes, spinach, and tomatoes.

Carbohydrates: Pasta, rice and couscous are good for you. I mentioned potatoes as a water based vegetable just in the preceding sentence. Sometime there is nothing better than a carb like a good ole baked potato.

Main Meal: Try to eat fish, chicken, turkey or lean beef the night before.

Breakfast: The morning of the match you may want to eat fruit, some carbs like cereal with very little milk, oatmeal, two pancakes or cream of wheat or cream of rice. Load up on water and sports drink.

Match Time: Continue to drink sports drinks and water on changeovers.

Of course, I ran into players who came from cultures that featured spicy food and were not used to having pre-match foods like the athletes have in the West. Vijay Amritraj and his brothers from Madras (now Chennai) where the hottest curry comes from obviously had a pre match meal that was not bland but those rice dishes provided the carbs they needed to play singles and doubles day after day in their early years. But, oh boy, were they unhappy if they couldn't find an Indian restaurant in whatever European or American city they happened to be in!

One needs to allow sufficient time to digest the food for it to be converted into fuel. The food that you eat tonight will be converted into fuel for tomorrow's match. If you are eating breakfast at seven a.m. this will be fueling your afternoon's match.

But diet is not the only thing you need to do to prepare. There is a routine that you can follow on the morning of the match that I find helps your body and all its working parts prepare for what you are about to put it through.

One of my first suggestions is this: When you wake up, get into a hot bath. You only need ten minutes to get your core temperature up. I prefer the soak in the hot tub to a shower but the least you can do is to have a hot shower. Then when you get out of the tub, towel off, get down on the floor on a dry towel and scoot yourself up near a wall. Put your legs up and prop them on the wall. The elevation will help drain the blood back into your core and this is good for your circulation. Your legs will not feel so heavy if you spend five minutes with your legs up on the wall. Then after five minutes you can begin stretches. Knees to chest, knees to the side, in other words stretch the hamstrings, quads, calf muscles, back, arms, etc. with these floor stretching drills.

Just before the match have a hot shower before you go on court. This shower also raises your core temperature. You will be warm to do your stretching. Muscles react the same way as would plastic. Cold plastic breaks. Heated plastic is malleable and will not break. Just like a muscle.

Rub a little analgesic balm into your shoulder, forearm, legs and lower back. This type of counter irritant applied topically actually will stay with you while you warm up. The effects will last and will help warm the muscles. It may also help with any aches and pains that you had before.

For foot care and the prevention of blisters, take a tube or jar of Vaseline and apply some topically with a thin coating to the balls of your feet, heels, toes and other areas where you will get friction. You can also sprinkle some baby powder on top of the Vaseline. Put your socks on, very carefully over your toes, making sure there are no wrinkles in the sock. If you have wrinkles, you might just get a blister, so smooth out the wrinkles. For those athletes that are prone to bruising of their feet, you may want to try a thicker sock such as Thorlo. Plan to bring an extra pair of socks and an extra pair of tennis shoes to change into for longer matches. Speaking of extra – you need to bring two backup tennis shirts and shorts. Throw in a warm up suit to wear after the match while you are cooling off.

When I mentioned the Vaseline and powder treatment it made me think of another method that I sometimes have used. I am referring to the use of pickle brine soaks. Salty brine has been proven as a skin toughening agent. Sailors, fishermen and others who are around salty water have tough hands that are conditioned and do not get blisters. During my days on the tour I would go to a deli and ask for the pickle brine that was left over from the sale of dill pickles. I would bring back the pickle brine to the arena and have the players soak their feet and hands in it. Ten minutes of soaking each day toughened up the players' feet and hands very fast.

Sometimes, on hard courts, in addition to the skin treatment of feet, there can be a need for additional padding. The stop and go movement on hard courts may require extra bandaging and padding over the first metatarsal head, toes, and heels.

Make sure your lacing pattern is even. Too tight laces in the mid-foot can bring on additional injury. If you don't have a prescribed orthotic you might try an off the shelf insole. The point here is that you need a good support system inside your shoe.

In hot and humid conditions you need to wear a hat. A white hat, which will reflect the heat, is preferable to a dark hat. Wear white clothing as it helps keep you cool. Clothing companies have newer fabrics that will wick the sweat away. Many companies have fabrics that provide a sun screen factor.

Playing outside you will need to apply a sun block of not less than 50 SPF. Even in overcast weather, one can get an adverse reaction to the rays which penetrate the clouds. Sun can really harm you. So take the proper precautions. After your match and practice, it is a good idea to cool down with a cold shower or ice bath. This will help to reduce inflammation and to relax your body.

Chapter C: Shoes

Before he got it right, Pete Sampras went through hell with his shoes. I remember he was playing in Lyon, a tournament he won in 1991 and 1992 before suffering with the US Davis Cup team in the same arena when they lost to France in the '92 Davis Cup Final, and towards the end of the week he came off court hurting bad. And no wonder. When I took his shoes off, his socks were red with blood. The skin on the top of his feet had been rubbed raw by the inside of the shoe. It was a bad fit. I got him in better shape for the final with ointments and extra padding but Pete knew that he would have long term problems if he didn't get himself a better shoe, which, of course, he did. Pete often came off court with burning feet but he never complained. He was a champion and just wanted to win. Each shoe fits each person differently. It was not a bad shoe but just a bad fit for Pete.

This was just one example of how important the shoe is to the tennis player so before we move on to the foot, let's take a look at what encases it and how you should go about selecting the right shoe for you. Think of them as your Michelin tires. They have to absorb the battering and swerving you put them through on the road. The tread has to be right and the pressure, too.

When you go to your pro shop or store looking for tennis shoes there are a few things that you need to keep in mind. You want to feel the shoes. Yep, you should squeeze them to see how they flex. Because the way they flex has a direct bearing on whether they are the right shoe for your foot.

If you look at a pair of your used tennis shoes, you should notice how the wear patterns are on the side of the shoes. Some tennis players will have the most wear on the outside of the heel or rear of the shoe. Others will show wear on the inner sides of their shoes. The first group is the supinators. Supinators usually have calluses on the first metatarsal head (commonly called the balls of your feet) and may have ankle problems. Pronators are the second group. The pronators have a flatter arch and a more flexible foot. They usually get blisters and calluses on the insides of their feet. Their arches may tire and have ankle instability. When you can see a shoe that has even wear, you have neutral feet. Neutrals do not have to be concerned as to how the shoe flexes.

Most people fall into the first two categories – pronators and supinators. They should consider a shoe that flexes at the ball of the foot and not at the arch. You need to pick up the shoe with both hands, right side up, holding the heel in one and the toe in the other. Squeeze your hands together. If the shoe folds at the ball of the foot, it's a good choice. If it flexes farther back, you need to find another shoe.

Although it may sound strange, I have seen athletes change from being one foot type (Pronator or Supinator) to the other. This happens many times when your foot changes from excessive play or daily activities. This is one good reason to have your feet checked out by a professional to see which foot type you are. In many cases it is the athletic trainer that can do this. Other professionals that can help you are a podiatrist or an orthotist.

Today's tennis shoes are the result of better research that the companies are investing in. When I first started in tennis there was not a good support system inside the shoe. The Brits would refer to these shoes as plimsoles. If you look at old pictures of Fred Perry or Brooke Shields' granddad, Frank Shields, both wore this type of shoe. Perry, a three time Wimbledon Champion back in the 1930's had terrible feet, probably as result of playing with so little support. In his later years he would come into the locker room at Wimbledon and I would work on his calluses. He was in his eighties by then. I wonder what state Rafa Nadal's feet will be in fifty years from now. Hopefully, better because of the improved design but one thing is sure – if Perry had played the type of physical game we see from Nadal and other modern day pros, he would not have had any feet left at all!

Then there was the Dunlop Volley which was a canvas shoe that the Aussies wore in colors of green and yellow or a royal blue and white – colorful but not very supportive. The Yanks wore the Converse Skid Grips, a canvas shoe. I will always remember the muscular Texan Cliff Richey, who used to get red in the face and sweat buckets, sloshing around in those Skid Grips. They were so soaked with sweat that at the end of the match he would squeeze the sweaty water out of them! Jimmy Connors wore Converse leather shoes that were so light that he wore them out in one or two matches. Connors liked a lightweight shoe which fitted his aggressive style. I never saw a player that spilled his guts on the court like Connors did. He never gave an excuse. He fought his opponent like no other player that I had seen. He played with more intensity than any player and never gave up. Winning was all that mattered to Jimmy. Defeat was a word he didn't understand. But, physically, he was a lightweight and so he could get away with a light shoe.

The other items that you would want to check out in a shoe are the heel collar which protects the Achilles tendon. If the heel collar is too high in the back you may get some irritation of the Achilles tendon. I have applied Skin Lube, a Cramer product, to the collar, to prevent friction between the collar and the tendon. You see more of this when the foot bed sits higher due to a newer orthotic. Arthur Ashe had problems in this area which is why he could be seen clomping around tournaments – or even up and down the Champs Elysees! – in wooden clogs like those they wear in Holland. They have no backs so Arthur's tender Achilles felt no pressure.

The heel counter in the rear of the shoe helps to stop the heel from slipping inside the shoe and stabilizes the rear of the foot. The stabilizing strap helps provide added side-to-side support in the front of the foot. The cup-sole wraps around the midsole to enhance side-to-side support. The midsole is the insole that runs the length of the shoe and cushions the blow of the playing surface. They're either made of ethyl vinyl acetate (EVA) and are more cushy or polyurethane (PU) and are more durable. You get a pair of these when you buy new shoes. However, custom made insoles or orthotics are better as they are made from a mold of your own feet. They follow the anatomical shape of YOUR feet and the changes that occur in your feet as time goes by.

The outsole is the actual tread of your shoes. One can learn a lot from seeing the wear that you put on this outsole. Here we are back to the different foot types: Supinated, Pronated and Neutral. There are different treads made to accommodate different playing surfaces and you should really take care if you are changing surfaces. If your club has hard courts and you have to go off and play on Har-Tru, the American clay, or on the red stuff over in Europe, you are going to need a different type of shoe. The same is true, of course, for grass – just in case you ever get invited to Wimbledon!

Your local pro shop should carry shoes with a tread that works best for that club's surface.

What's a Shoe Worth?

Numerous times on the tour a player finds himself in a situation where his agent – thinking money first as he is supposed to – gets him a shoe deal. But sometimes the shoe deal does not work out because that company does not produce a model which works for that particular player. Their shoe does not flex the way it should. And so, the deal is made and the player is not happy. Nowadays, most companies will custom build a shoe for their name players but for youngsters coming onto the tour without proper representation or parents who don't understand the importance of footwear, the problem remains. A decade or so ago South American players from poor backgrounds used to arrive on the tour with hammer toes – a tell tale sign of having been made to play in shoes that were too small for them because they couldn't afford new ones. Some had been made to play in their brother's shoes. So the toes became crunched together and curled under – becoming hammer toes. Sometimes they needed to be surgically treated.

But occasionally, foot problems could be alleviated by the somewhat simpler method of conducting surgery on the shoe rather than the foot! Andre Agassi was one player who frequently had blisters on his little toe which can be really painful. There were many times that I would take a scalpel and make tiny little cuts along the seam just above where the little toe would rub against the leather. It just made a little more room and released the pressure. I first used this method with baseball players in the days when they were playing in kangaroo leather shoes. Another way of stretching a leather shoe to make it a little roomier without going up a size is to use a shoe tree, preferably one of those wooden shoe trees you get if you buy a terribly expensive pair of shoes in New York or London. But cheaper ones can be effective, too!

It is all about making the shoe adapt to your foot and of course, choosing the right type of shoe for you. There are no hard and fast rules and some players have stepped out of the shoe box, if you like, and just done what seemed right for them. Martin Jaite, the fine little player from Argentina who went on to captain his country's Davis Cup team, was one. Unlike some of the South Americans, Jaite had the luxury of making his own decisions about footwear and made an unusual choice. His game was based on speed and running, primarily on clay, so he wore running shoes. Not to be recommended for everyone but it worked for him.

I recall several players that would bitch and complain about the shoe that they were obligated to wear. The shoes just hurt their feet. It got so bad that the money was not important enough to negate how the shoe felt and how it was to compete in.

One time I even witnessed a player throw his shoes at his agent because he was so pissed off the way the shoes hurt his feet! The money is not worth it if your feet hurt.

Every tiny advantage counts on the pro tour these days and if a player feels he moves better with a certain type of shoe it is worth dropping a few thousand dollars on the contract rather than lose confidence in matches. For the amateur player, the thinking should be in reverse. Nobody will be paying you to wear the shoe but, if you are serious about your game, don't let money become a factor if you can afford the extra dollar. Get the shoe that fits you, even if it is more expensive.

Parents of budding young players really should take this very seriously. If the money is available, they should get their youngster fitted with proper orthotics, just like the pros do. Most of the top pros order a dozen pairs at the start of the year so as to be well stocked. Glenn Cumberland of Bloomfield Hills, Michigan is the orthotist I trust most in this field. He has been supplying me and players on the tour since 1985. Glenn uses a foam impression system that really helps support the foot. I use them because, although I may not run around much, I stand around all day and feet complain about that, too!

Chapter D: The Foot

Inevitably, tennis players suffer from foot problems. Feet take a pounding on any type of surface but with more play on hard courts these days; it almost becomes a question of "Feet First!" when it comes to treating the routine problems.

I will try to take you through some of the ways you can ease those problems and maybe succeed in avoiding some of them.

With all injuries you need to use ice to control swelling and pain. Always, if pain persists, you need to contact your physician.

With most of these tennis injuries we are dealing with soft tissue. A bursa is a soft tissue sac of synovial fluid where tendons slide over bony prominences. External pressure from a poorly fitting tennis shoe may cause inflammation, resulting in bursitis and swelling, a hot feeling in the tissue and of course, pain.

Bursitis

I don't see this condition so much with junior tennis players or pro tour players. I do see this sometimes in older country club tennis players.

The bursa (between the Achilles tendon insertion and the calcaneus bone and the posterior aspect of the talus bone) gets a lot of irritation during a tennis match. This is localized pain in soft tissue just in front of the Achilles tendon. Pain is usually present with plantar flexion and pushing off when you are serving and then running to the net. This bursitis is difficult to treat (rest from tennis activity, ice packs, super-pulsed low level laser, whirlpools baths, electrical therapy and occasionally a short leg walking cast for complete rest) but you need to exhaust all means of treatment if you eventually want to get back on the court. At times, a bursitis may develop between the Achilles tendon and the overlying skin. This bursitis is related to the type of tennis shoe that you are wearing. Sometime you have to "doctor" your shoe as I did with Agassi. You may have something in the rear compartment (shoe collar) of the shoe that is irritating your Achilles tendon and the heel. I have used heel cups to cradle the heel and rear foot and this will take the pressure off the heel and calcaneus bone. With a bunion sometimes a bursitis may develop over the bony prominence. The tennis player will have to address this with a change in tennis shoes. Maybe a tennis shoe that has "room" to accommodate this bony part of his or her foot. Some players will have to consult a podiatrist or a orthopaedist that specializes in foot and ankle conditions.

Callus

I have always helped tennis players with the management of this condition. A callus is an area of thickened skin overlying a bony prominence. Usually there is abnormal pressure between the tennis shoe and the bony protrusion. You need to file the callus down each week with a pumice stone, soak the feet in pickle brine as the brine helps to treat and toughen the calluses and the skin on the feet. I have seen calluses that were so thick that they even developed a blister under the callus. If that happens, you have to have the blister drained with a sterile syringe to remove the pressure from the liquid buildup. Another option for the blister is to drain it with a sterile needle. Puncturing it will speed the healing process. First sterilize your foot and then use a needle with alcohol. At the edge of the blister right where it meets the skin make a tiny hole and let the fluid leak out. Then apply some antibiotic ointment to prevent infection. Cover the blister with Cover-Roll stretch by BSN Medical adhesive dressing and leave it there. In three days the dead skin will work itself loose, the new skin underneath will have had a chance to toughen up.

Additionally, you can cover this with Second Skin if the area is still tender. The worst foot blister that I have seen in the past ten years was a blister that developed on the foot of the Colombian, Alejandro Falla. Alejandro was playing on one of the side courts at the Canadian Open a few years ago. I was summoned to his court. When we removed his shoe and sock, the sock was filled with blood. He had a blister about the size of a silver dollar right on his first metatarsal head or what many would call the ball of his foot. This area is very prone to friction. The skin came off in one huge piece of callus. The blood was pouring out of this wound. I was able to bandage and pad this up but Alejandro had lots of pain to deal with. The super pulsed low level laser speeds up the healing process with a few treatments to the blister/wound.

The plantar fascia is a dense fibrous band that runs from the heel bone (calcaneal tuberosity) along the plantar surface of the foot and inserts on the plantar surface of the metatarsal heads. In other words, the plantar fascia is simply a thick band that connects the heel bone to the ball of your foot. When you get up in the morning you need to get into a hot tub and soak your feet in hot water. Then sit down, put a Heineken (or a Coke) bottle on the floor, and roll the bottom of your foot back and forth. You don't have to put too much downward pressure. This fascia can become irritated from overuse from tennis activity and may be most painful to players that have a high arch (Cavus feet). You get up in the morning and you are hobbling around like an old man. It feels like you are stepping on tacks. Pain is most severe at the calcaneal tuberosity but may spread along the course of the fascia. Occasionally, in chronic cases the fascia calcifies at its insertion on the heel bone resulting in a heel spur. Treatment includes padding on the heel, an orthosis, seeing a podiatrist or orthopaedist that specializes in foot and ankle conditions and rest. I have had success treating this condition with a super pulsed low level laser. The soft tissue on the heel may be injured from direct trauma (stone bruise). Super-pulsed low level therapeutic laser also addresses the pain in this condition.

With the stop and go of your movements on the tennis courts the toes take a beating. The great toe (first toe or big toe) gets bruised when you stop short and the foot jams into the toe box. It helps a lot to always have your toenails trimmed straight across, so that the corners clear the fold of skin at the edges. This will prevent you from having ingrown toenails. The other suggestion to prevent this bruising is to place lamb's wool in the toe box. This will give the toes some cushion when the foot jams forward in the tennis shoe. Many times the problem is from an undersized tennis shoe. As you move on the court your foot spreads out and swells up slightly. Your tennis shoes should be one size larger than your street shoes. Sizes vary from brand to brand so always try on a new tennis shoe. If you notice that your toenail, especially on your big toe, is getting bruised from just the movement on the tennis court, the tennis shoes are too small. I have even seen this with shoes mismarked. You see the size printed on the inside of the tennis shoes but it had been incorrectly marked.

With the bruising of the toenails you may get some bleeding under the toenail. To relieve this you need to get a paper clip and with a pair of pliers, straighten out the paper clip into a long piece of metal. Grasp the end of the metal end of the straightened out paper clips with the pliers. Hold it over a kitchen stove burner until it is red hot. Then push it through the nail where you see the pooling of blood under the nail. Soon as the paper clip melts through the nail the blood will drain out of the opening. When that blood seeps out you are going to feel very good with this pain release. Sooooo good! You can also use this same procedure for blood under a fingernail. It works!

There are some tennis players that have a larger 2nd toe. This second toe is longer than the Great toe. Since most tennis shoes normally accommodate the 1st toe being the longest, it is difficult finding a shoe that addresses a player with a longer 2nd toe. This condition is referred to as a Morton's toe. It affects the area between the 2nd and 3rd toes. The nerve can get inflamed and now this becomes a plantar neuroma. You can get some pain relief by placing a pad on the bottom of the foot, right behind that area that hurts. The pad creates a bit of an arch, which raises your foot and makes it narrower, further reducing pressure on the aching nerve. You can buy these metatarsal pads at your pharmacy or consult your foot and ankle specialist. Please don't try to play with pain.

Athlete's Foot

To prevent athlete's foot you should wash and dry your feet immediately after a match or practice. Make sure you dry between the toes. Then apply foot powder or baby powder to the bottoms of your feet and between the toes. Sprinkle some powder inside your shoes. Change into a pair of clean, dry socks. Dry your shoes out after practice and matches. Loosen up the shoe laces and bring the shoe tongue out so it can dry. Try to alternate wearing your tennis shoes with a second pair. You never want to wear wet shoes. Wear dry shoes! Wear tennis shoes that breathe well. Try to wear tennis shoes that are made with mesh and air vents. Wear leather street shoes, not synthetics. Your socks should be made of acrylic or cool-max or even better, Thorlo socks. They wick moisture away from your feet. Cotton absorbs sweat but does not evaporate the sweat. Wear flip flops around the locker room, your hotel room and especially the shower room! You need to avoid fungal infections. The surfaces in the hotel floor, locker room and shower room floor are full of this fungus. Please be careful with this condition. If you do develop Athlete's foot you can treat it yourself. See your pharmacist for the anti-fungal creams and sprays that he or she recommends. If your condition does not improve, you need to see a dermatologist. Out-of control Athlete's foot can be so painful that it will be hard to bear weight.

These are the most common foot problems. I thought I would share these little tidbits in hope that you can use them.

Chapter E: The Ankle

In all my years, I have dealt with all kinds of injuries as a health care provider. But nothing has been as constant as ankle injuries which crop up relentlessly on both the men's and women's tennis tours. With all the directions that the ankle moves on the tennis court it is amazing how special this structure is.

Years ago, many tennis courts of India were made of dung and had small divots in the surface. This led to many sprains. Even on hard courts, a player can always step on a ball or in doubles play, step on his partner's foot, and turn the ankle over. Ankle sprains account for as much as one-fifth of the injuries seen in training rooms on the ATP tour.

I always told my players that if you roll an ankle please do not take the tennis shoe off. Go in the opposite direction – tighten up the laces. If you do take the tennis shoe off, the ankle will immediately swell up. You need to have that compression on the foot and ankle. Leave it on until the athletic trainer gets to you. He or she will know how to manage the injured ankle. I have even told players that if you are alone, with no athletic trainer on site, you are better off submerging the whole shoe, encasing the foot, in a bucket or small waste can filled with ice and water. Leave the shoe in the ice for twenty minutes. Take it out for twenty minutes and elevate the ankle to a height where the ankle is higher than your hips and your heart. After an hour of this treatment, get yourself to a hospital emergency room for x-rays.

I feel that either you are going to sprain the ankle or fracture the ankle. Get yourself to a hospital and have your ankle x-rayed. Boris Becker's famous ankle sprain in the 1985 Wimbledon Championships did not appear to be so swollen. He was able to bear weight and I could tape the ankle in a way that he could continue to play. I treated him almost around the clock that fortnight. He was very responsive to the treatment and was able to go on to win the Championships.

Ankle sprains are graded one, two or three. The tennis player gently twists his ankle, stretching the ligaments, with no real tearing. That would be a mild, or grade 1) sprain. A tennis player who lunges out over a carelessly planted foot, partially tearing the fibers of the ligament, is a moderate or a grade 2) sprain. When the player jumps and lands on another player's foot or on a tennis ball, twisting and tearing all the fibers, this is a severe or grade 3) sprain. A moderate sprain requires aggressive treatment and a severe sprain requires a cast and/or further surgical options.

If your ankle is treated correctly you can avoid down time and be able to return to competition in a few weeks. If you don't take care of this injury properly, you could be out of action for several months. Always have the ankle medically checked unless it is a very mild sprain. Most ankle sprains that I have seen happen when you roll the outside part of your ankle and sprain the ligaments. There's swelling and pain on the outside of the ankle and black and bluish coloring accompanying the ankle. This is blood from the broken vessels flowing downward due to gravity.

Sometime, I will see a player sprain the inside of their ankle. It's not very common but it happens. You usually get a fracture with this injury. The inside ligament is stronger than the inside bone. It can pull off a bone fragment at its attachment. Again get the x-ray to know what you are dealing with.

The forward sprain results when the forefoot flips you and you roll over your toes. The tendons in the forefoot are pulled and your capsule in your ankle ruptures. This capsule holds the ankle's structure and acts as a stabilizer. The recovery time for this sprain is long.

R.I.C.E .is the proper treatment for an acutely sprained ankle.

REST

ICE

COMPRESSION

ELEVATION

I want to emphasize again – if you roll an ankle please do not take the tennis shoe off. Go in the opposite direction – tighten up the laces. If you do take the tennis shoe off, the ankle will immediately swell up. You need to have that COMPRESSION on the foot and ankle. Leave it on until the athletic trainer gets to you. He or she will know how to manage the injured ankle. And remember, if you are alone, with no athletic trainer on site, you are better off submerging the whole shoe. Leave the shoe in the ICE for twenty minutes. Take it out for twenty minutes and ELEVATE the ankle to a height where the ankle is higher than your hips and your heart. After an hour of this treatment, get yourself to a hospital emergency room for x-rays.

As a tennis player you need to do the necessary things to recover from this injury. Stay off the ankle and get REST. Don't continue to try to play. Seek medical advice. ICE your ankle every twenty minutes for the first seventy-two hours. Have a COMPRESSION bandage on your ankle. ELEVATE your ankle. Continue this procedure throughout your recovery period.

Exercises

Before one begins an exercise program it is necessary to check with your physician.

After an ankle injury you should start doing some exercises to get some circulation in your ankle. You can begin by sitting on a table or a counter, something high that your legs can dangle. Try crossing your injured leg over the other leg at the knee. I want you to picture yourself drawing with your big toe, the letters of the alphabet. Now, your big toe is the pointer, you need to trace the capital letters of the alphabet from A to Z. Your Great Toe needs to be rigid. The motion comes from the ankle. Perform this exercise every hour while you are up and about. You will see the letters get larger in size as your range of motion increases.

Figure 1: Ankle Recovery Alphabet Range of Motion

Depending on how serious your injury is, you need to try bearing weight as soon as you can. It's a slow process. If you cannot bear weight, you'll have to get crutches. As you use the crutches, put a little weight on your ankle to try the crutches out. Don't bear weight until you can walk normally. When you get your range of motion back from the alphabet exercises that you've done, you can start getting the ankle strong with the next exercises, starting with the lift.

For an ankle lift, take a piece of rope about one and a half feet long, and either tie a five pound weight to each end or loop the rope around a ten pound weight. You can sit on a table high enough that you can swing your legs and dangle your feet without touching the floor and drop the rope over the top of the midfoot while wearing tennis shoes. Lift the weight with your ankle until you reach tiredness in your ankle. Hang in there!

Figure 2: Ankle Lift

For an ankle-turn, sit on a table, take a four foot rope, put it under the arch of the shoe of the injured foot, and hold the ends of the rope at about knee height. Then turn your ankle as far as it will go to the inside. Pull on part of the rope and force that ankle to the outside. Here you are working against the resistance of the rope. Now, when your foot is all the way out, pull on the outside part of the rope as you bring your foot back to the inside. You are working against resistance. Keep the inward and outward movements going until your ankle is flat out tired.

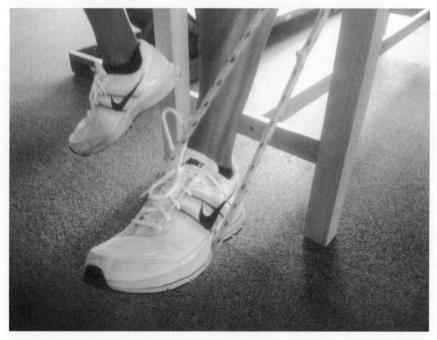

Figure 3: Ankle Turn

For the foot-lift outward, check this out: while sitting on a table, hang a weight on the top of your midfoot, point your foot up, and turn your ankle as far as it will go to the outside. Do as many reps as possible Begin with five pound dumbbell and progress to a heavier dumbbell.

Figure 4: Foot Lift Outward

For the foot-lift-inward, check this out, you are sitting on a table, hang a weight on the midfoot, you need to point your foot up, and turn your ankle as far as it will go toward the inside. Do as many reps as possible. Here you need to begin with a five pound dumbbell and progress to a heavier dumbbell(s).

Figure 5:   Foot Lift Inward Toe

For the toe-raise, you'll need to stand on your toes for ten seconds and then come down flat on the floor. Do the reps until you're tired in your calf muscles. As the calf muscles strengthen, you can put all of your weight on the injured foot and keep the other leg off the floor. If you hold dumbbells as added weight, you can get a different effect. Try the stronger leg for balance, lift with the injured calf.

Figure 6: Toe Raise

For the heel drop, you'll stand with your forefeet (toes and forward part of your foot on a raised surface (phone book or curb or short platform are good), pretend you do a back dive off a diving board. You need to let your weight take your heels down below the level of the surface so that the back of your calf is stretched. Hold for ten to fifteen seconds and come back up. Repeat until your calf is tired. When you see progress in your injury (that it is healing and getting stronger), try bearing weight on the injured ankle.

Figure 7: Heel Drop

The exercises here have been proven to be good and useful. They are used on the ATP tour by the players. They need to be done until you feel your muscles are totally tired. You will also need to work on your balance. Try balancing on one foot and then the other. Close your eyes and balance. If you have problems getting back your strength you should see an athletic trainer to continue the rehabilitation.

Each of these exercises should be done to the point of total muscle fatigue, so that you can't do even one more. Balancing is important in re-training an injured ankle to sense where the foot is in relation to the ground. Practice by balancing on one foot with your arms stretched out to the sides until you lose balance or become fatigued. When your ankle gets better, do this exercise with your eyes closed. If the sprain is severe or if you need to return to play you should consider a good tennis related physical therapy program. All of the exercises that I mentioned can be done on machines, which are much more effective than weights and pieces of rope.

For balance-training you can stand on a balancing board, which is a board that rests on a cylinder and allows you to roll back and forth. These exercises can be combined with super pulsed low level laser therapy, range of motion exercises and soft tissue massage.

I also like to include whirlpool baths. The temperature of the water should not be more than one hundred five degrees. The duration of hydrotherapy treatment should not exceed eight minutes. We have had real good response with these rehabilitation protocols on the ATP Tour.

On the tour, ankle taping is a normal procedure that you will see each day. It is used as a preventative treatment for protecting the ankle from all the overuse that it is asked to do.

Ankle taping is used as a treatment for already injured ankles as well. The ATP athletic trainers go through miles and miles of adhesive tape each year. The downside to using tape is that after one hour of practice and match play, the adhesive tape begins to lose its tensile strength. Sweat breaks down the adhesive and sometime the athletic trainer has to come out and re-tape the ankle.

An ankle brace is an alternative to ankle taping. New Options Sports have supplied the ATP Tour since 1979 with their models of ankle braces as well as neoprene sleeves, wraps and other braces for other body parts. The player can apply the correct tension as the practice session or match progresses.

In tennis an ankle can break if it is turned severely with great force. This happens when a player goes for a shot and steps on a tennis ball or in doubles play, going wide, and steps on his partner's foot. He turns the ankle with the force of his full weight. If the player is going for a ball and suddenly changes direction, he can suffer a fractured ankle. Common signs of a broken ankle, which is often difficult to spot, include a recurrent diffuse ache in the ankle that increases with exercise; swelling after exercise, followed by pain free periods; limited movement; and ankle bruising. You need a sports medicine physician that can put you in the right direction along with a sports medicine therapist to administer your rehabilitation. We all agree on one thing: You want to be able to return to the tennis courts in a safe, timely manner. Tennis is your passion!

Chapter F: Lower Leg Conditions in Tennis

No matter what level of tennis player you are dealing with, they all suffer from injuries to the calf or lower leg at some time or another. In most cases the first place that you have to look for symptoms is the player's feet. They are almost always the bad guy behind shin and lower leg pain. Almost all the pain that occurs on the inner side of the shin bone is due to improper foot strike – the way the foot hits the ground when you run around the court. This is an overuse injury syndrome

The symptoms depend on the amount of stress you place on your legs and the problems you have with your foot strike. I have seen so many players suffer with lower leg pain from shin splints to stress fractures to chronic calf cramping.

Inactive individuals with severe foot abnormality have no leg pain, on the other hand, a tennis player that is always busting his butt to get to the ball and has mild foot abnormality, can suffer from shin pain quite badly.

Shin Splints

Pains on the inner side of the shin, usually in the muscles near the shin bone. Tennis players complain of this pain most when they play on hard courts. Pain is felt on the middle third of the shin bone. I've heard of treatment ranging from a tobacco poltice (used because of its nicotine content) to physical therapy, anything to lessen the pain. I've tried taping a band two inches above the ankle. This seems to help in most cases. You need to seek medical advice from your physician. A custom made orthotic has been the main form of treatment and prevention for this condition. The orthotic prevents excessive pronation and pull on the tendon.

Glenn Cumberland has helped many tennis players over the years, custom fitting them with orthotics. The ATP Tour has used his service since 1985. It has been my experience that many cases of shin splints result when the tennis player transitions from playing on clay courts to playing on hard courts. Professional tennis players take this transition in stride going from one season to the next and the surface changes that are part of the game. Peter Fleming was one of those players that had to deal with shin splints during his career from time to time. But I never saw a player withdraw from playing with this condition. We would just administer treatment to the shin (hydrotherapy, electrical therapy, laser therapy, heat packs prior to playing, taping, and ice packs post match) and the player would go out and play.

If the twisting (and over stressing) of the shinbone is severe and is repeated enough times, the bone will crack. Many junior players develop stress fractures. Their growth plates are open, bones are not fully developed, and pain is felt in the foot and lower leg. The overuse is present when juniors are practicing and playing up to six hours each day which is far too much.

We learn more each year how to prevent this syndrome. As I mentioned before, a good foot bed or orthotic, can correct this excessive pronation but we need to use more common sense in how much time the juniors are asked to spend on the courts. So, using the orthotic is only one part of dealing with this overuse, the other is to come to terms with a sensible playing time line.

Stress Fractures

They are tender before they're painful and the area of tenderness is well-defined. At the beginning your leg might hurt when you put your socks on but it might not hurt when you play tennis. If you run your fingers down the shin bone and feel a spot the size of a fifty cent coin you might be concerned. However, if you move your finger up an inch or down an inch from the spot, and there is no pain, there is no reason to worry. The sooner you recognize the tender spot the sooner you can address the stress fracture or the possibility of a stress fracture. You have to stay off of it and let the bone heal. In the last two years I have had success in the bone healing process by using my super pulsed low level laser on these conditions.

The photons of light going into the bone cells activate the production of Adenosine Tri-phosphate (ATP), increasing blood flow, and decreasing the inflammation and healing the bone.

You still need to concentrate on the rest of your fitness. Your upper body needs exercise, so don't neglect it. You need to do your cardio. The trick is to find a level of activity that is as strenuous as possible and the same time pain free. Then you're accomplishing both. You are treating the stress fracture, because the way to promote healing is to maintain a pain free level of activity and continuing your conditioning, pushing the bone to become stronger. When you're able to resume the level of activity that caused the problem in the first place the bone will be able to handle the stress.

Muscle Strains

Tears commonly occur in the major muscles of the calf, the Gastrocnemius and Soleus. These muscles help you in tennis to push off and to generally get around the court. Tennis leg is one of these strains that we deal with many times with the country club tennis players and sometimes the pro tour player. Tennis leg injury usually occurs when there has not been a proper or long enough warmup. The wall push-up and the toe raise should be done on the court against a fence.

When you do have an injury to the calf and lower leg muscles, R.I.C.E. is indicated. After seventy-two hours you may begin a gentle, gradual stretching program. For the calf, you need to do the wall push up facing the wall or the fence on the tennis court. Put one foot as far from a wall or fence as possible and keep your back heel flat on the ground and your other leg a few inches from the wall or fence. Your elbows need to be bent and then you lean into the wall and support yourself with your hands, but don't let your back heel come off the ground. Hold stretch for ten to fifteen seconds and push back up. Reverse legs and repeat. After the calf muscles are stretched you need to do the toe raises to strengthen these muscles.

Figure 8: Wall Pushup

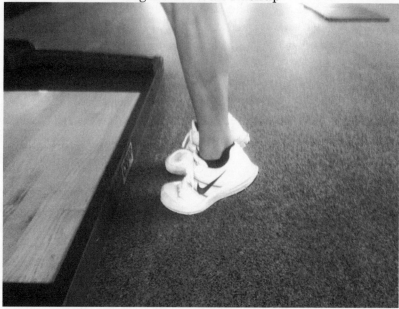

Figure 9: Toe Raise

With your feet pointing straight ahead, rise up on to your toes-with your knees straight to strengthen the gastrocnemius or with your knees bent to strengthen the soleus. Rise up, hold the position for a few seconds, then let down. Keep repeating the exercise until you get tired, then do it one more time. Gradually increase the number of toe raises until you're doing three sets of twenty each-that's a reasonable goal. Balancing on your toes is a good way to strengthen the calf muscles as well as this provides a good workout for the muscles around the ankle. With this exercise it does not matter if your knee is straight or bent, it's your choice which calf muscle you prefer to exercise. Your doctor may recommend a night splint. This holds the ankle at a right angle with a constant stretch.

Stand on your toes for ten seconds and then come down flat on the floor. Repeat until you feel real fatigue in your calf muscles. As the calf muscles begin to strengthen, you can put all of your weight on the affected leg and keep the other leg off the floor. Then you can hold dumbbells or a barbell to increase your body weight. Use the unaffected leg for balance, but do all the lifting with the affected calf.

Calf Cramps

Usually occur after stressful exercise. The condition may be triggered by an electrolyte imbalance, improper diet, lack of conditioning, illness or dehydration. The interesting thing here is that tennis players are pretty good about hydrating their bodies and eating the right foods that contain important electrolytes. Players are getting better each year at preparing properly. They pre-hydrate the night before, the day of the match, during the match and re-hydrate after the match. So, I go back to a previous statement that I made of how tennis players deal with stress. I do feel that stress has a lot to do with cramping. I think there are some players that deal with stress better than others. Shuzo Matsuoko's cramping during his US Open match on the Grandstand Court was one of the most severe cases witnessed in modern times. This case really changed the thinking of how to deal with this condition.

Page 154

The clearest evidence of why I feel stress plays such an important part in cramps is this: Players rarely cramp in practice, no matter how long they are on court. They only cramp in match play. If you are on court and you feel your lower leg muscles twitching, go to the fence and use it for the wall push-ups. I also recommend an ice cup massage for easing the cramp. Have Styrofoam cups filled with water placed overnight in the freezer. When the cups are frozen, peel some of the Styrofoam down to where you have a frozen ice edge. Rub the ice edge on the muscle until the skin is pink. When the skin is turning pink to red, the cramping is lessened.

Achilles Tendon

The largest tendon in the body. Some players develop Achilles tendinitis when they have excessive pronation of the ankle and foot. If they have this condition and they are jumping around on the courts, chasing down balls, etc, it can get worse. This tendinitis usually starts insidiously and then feeds on itself. You need to break the cycle of injury before it has a chance to settle in. If you notice your tendon hurting after a match, stretch well and ice the area to decrease the blood flow. To stretch, stand with your foot pointed straight ahead, keep your heel on the ground, and slowly bend your body forward over your ankle. You'll feel the tug in your Achilles tendon. Keeping your knee straight stretches the gastrocnemius, the large muscle in the calf as well. Bending the knee stretches the small muscle, the soleus. Don't practice the next day as you normally do. Do half as much and then stretch and ice as before. Most likely the problem will then go away. With ankle sprains, it's crucial to catch the problem immediately. Don't ignore it. Without you stretching and icing, it will be a pain in the calf! You need to rest and ice this tendon and use anti-inflammatory medication to relieve the pain and swelling. Stretch the tendon as well with wall push-ups or heel drops and toe raises.

Figure 10: Heel Drop

With the heel-drop, you'll stand with your toes and forward part of your foot on a raised surface (phone book, curb or short platform are good), pretend you do a back flip off a diving board. You need to let your weight take your heels down below the level of the surface so that the back of your calf is stretched. Hold for ten to fifteen seconds and come back up. Repeat until your calf is tired. When you see progress in your injury (that it is healing and getting stronger), try bearing weight on the injured ankle.

Achilles Tendon Rupture

Sometimes seen on the pro circuit, although I have seen only two in the past ten years, it is an item that I would like to comment on. An Achilles tendon rupture is a complete tear of the Achilles tendon. Sometimes called the heel cord, is the tendon attachment of the calf muscles, from the leg and knee to the heel bone. With the rupture, there is loss of continuity between the calf muscles and the heel bone and thus loss of function of the calf muscles. The function of the calf muscles is to forcefully push the front of the foot down (that is like when you're standing on your toes or when you are pushing off when walking, running or jumping) In other words, it's all what you do when you are playing tennis. A lot of times it will be a pop or a rip at the back of the heel that you will feel. Weakness in the foot, tenderness and swelling of the tendon and change of color in the skin on the tendon are signs of this injury. You need to grasp the tendon and feel if there is a separation in the tendon, a loss of firm fullness when you push on the area. Again, to prevent this, you need to always stretch the tendon. You should ice after activity, have the tendon taped with a protective strapping and if you have Achilles tendinitis, get it treated and rehabilitated. Once the tendon is ruptured you need to see your physician for an evaluation. Sometimes this injury requires surgery. If it does not require surgery, the recovery time is four to nine weeks. You will also need to have rehabilitation. Your physician can set that up for you.

The Popliteus tendon runs parallel to the Achilles tendon on the inside of the leg. When you get pain and tenderness in the back of the knee, a cracking sound when it moved, or pain while standing with a bent leg, well, that's popliteus tendinitis. You need to ice it after activity and get some whirlpool every morning on it when you wake up. Be sure to see your physician and have him refer you to a sports medicine therapist for your rehabilitation.

If you fracture either the shinbone (Tibia) or the smaller bone (Fibula), you will be under a physician's care initially. Both bones heal slowly and need some assistance. Here, I have used my super pulsed low level laser to increase the inducible nitric oxide synthase levels and ATP in the bone cells. This promotes better circulation in the lower leg and speeds up the bone healing.

Tennis Leg

A reminder: the failure to warm up properly contributes to tennis leg. This injury results when tennis players try to cut corners. They just show up without stretching properly and hydrating adequately and so stress their muscles and joints. I see it so often now that I am treating club players in my practice. A muscle that is not warmed up is just waiting to be strained. Tennis leg is what we call a calf muscle or a tendon that is torn when the player rushes the net. The pain is intense and it feels like the back of your calf was hit by a rock. This injury can be avoided with an adequate warm-up and stretching program along with good nutrition and proper hydration.

Chapter G: Assorted Tennis Injuries

The body has many moving parts and the game of tennis requires you to move an awful lot of them! Each stroke brings different muscles into play as you respond to shots that require varying aspects of footwork from speed to positioning. And that is just on court. As we will see you can even injure yourself in bed! In trying to kick the sheets out in a well made bed, (to free my feet), I strained my lower leg and ankle. So, let's take a detailed look at the long list of assorted injuries that a tennis player may have to deal with.

Neck Pain

You should see your physician if you have the following neck pain symptoms: pain that radiates down your arm, numbness or tingling in your arms weakness in your arm (cannot grasp or hold with hand or arm), or extreme pain that gets sharply worse with coughing or sneezing.

Looking up to hit an overhead or a serve can pull a neck muscle. This injury, called wry neck, is the same pain that you may feel when you wake up and feel you can only turn your head in one direction. This example of neck pain happened to Goran Ivanisevic in the 1996 Lipton Championships at Key Biscayne in Miami. Goran woke up and could not move his head. His neck muscles were stiff and in spasm. He attempted to go on the court and play against Andre Agassi but only lasted three games and had to retire. With this you need to ice the stiff side and then gently stretch the neck away from the stiff side. In other words, if your right side is stiff, try to place your left ear on your shoulder. The best way to prevent a neck injury is to strengthen your neck muscles.

Neck Strengthening Exercises

Neck Tilt Against Resistance: You tilt your head to the right while applying resistance with your right hand, hold for twenty seconds. Next tilt your head to the left and resist with your left hand for twenty seconds. Do same exercise, tilting your head forward and backward. For the stiff neck you need to stretch out the muscles so they can't stay in spasm. Your neck goes in six directions: forward, chin on chest, backward, looking at the ceiling, to either side, ear to shoulder and it twists, looking over shoulder. Those are the directions to stretch, opposite from the way your neck is tilted. If you wake up and you are looking over your right shoulder, stretch by turning to the left. If your ear is tilted toward your left shoulder, tilt to the right. All of these motions should be long and slow. You can contract and relax stretch your neck as well. Stretch, then push the other way against your own arm, then stretch some more. Isometric exercises are easy. Push your head and neck against the resistance of your arm.

Figure 11: Neck Tilt Against Resistance

Before one begins using heavy weights it is necessary to check with your physican.

Shoulder Shrug with Barbell: Hold barbell with fifty to one hundred pounds of weight straight down in front of you with your elbows locked. Shrug your shoulders and hold for five seconds. You do five repetitions for five sets. This strengthens trapezius muscle in neck. Beginners should use less weight and build up slowly to fifty to one hundred pounds of weight. If this weight is too difficult go with less weight.

Figure 12: Shoulder Shrug with Barbell

Figure 13: Shoulder Shrug with Barbell

Shoulder Shrug: You lift shoulders up to ears and then drop them as low as they can go. Do five reps.

Figure 14: Shoulder Shrug

Figure 15: Shoulder Shrug Up

Trapezius Stretch: It's where you sit on a bench and hold the bench with the hand of the painful side. Now bend your trunk and your head to the opposite side. Bend your neck away and a little bit forward from the side that hurts. Long, slow stretches will unknot the muscle.

Figure 16: Trapezius Stretch

Chin Jut: You are sitting down, look slowly to the side, over one shoulder and then over the other shoulder. Do this five times back and forth. Jut your chin forward and back five times.

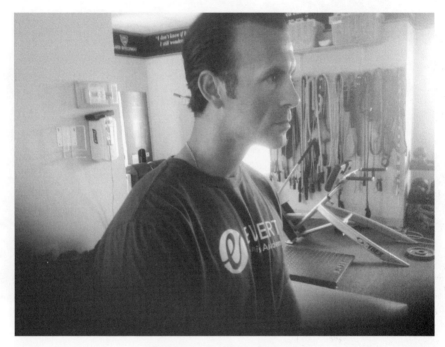

Figure 17: Chin Jut

Chin Drop: you drop chin to chest. Move chin in a semicircle from shoulder to shoulder five times.

Figure 18: Chin Drop

Shoulder Roll: Roll shoulders by making a circle. Lift both shoulders and roll them forward five times, then lift and roll them backward five times.

Figure 19: Shoulder Roll

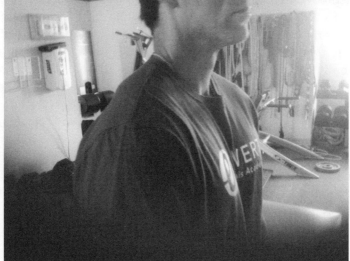

Figure 20: Shoulder Roll 2

Tennis Elbow

The correct name for this condition is elbow tendonitis or in the medical world as lateral epicondylitis. This condition results when the lateral muscles and tendons in the outside of the forearm have not been strengthened enough to handle the wear and tear of hitting tennis balls.

I believe that micro tears in the tendon origin, caused by heavy or repetitive activity, will aggravate tennis elbow.

When a player's timing is off, maybe hitting the backhand late, there is stress on the lateral extensor muscles. I see this condition many times when I treat club players. I do not see this too often with professional players as their timing is almost perfect and their arm muscles are strong and flexible. The extensor muscles can be strengthened by some exercises in this chapter. To further strengthen the extensors there is a product called the EZelbow that can prevent further injury for activities, treat the symptoms with heat compression therapy, Xtensor exercise, targeted acupressure and cold compression.

I have seen professional players get pain on the inside of their elbow. Stan Smith had this pain in the early 70s but had it corrected with therapy. Maria Bueno had the classic tennis elbow and it severely hampered her time with World Team Tennis towards the end of her career. Every time a player hits the ball the elbow ends up absorbing most of the shock. The player may be a little late in hitting the ball because of its speed. When you develop tennis elbow it seems that everyday activities irritate the elbow. You need to always seek medical attention for this condition to get a proper diagnosis for treatment. Epicondylitis has an average duration of 12 to 15 months with many recurrences and setbacks along the way. The proper treatment of tennis elbow is an exercise program with EZelbow system and the Xtensor Hand Exerciser and with light weights to strengthen elbow muscles and tendons. Again, you will need a five pound dumbbell for men and a two and a half pound dumbbell for women. You can increase the weight as you get these areas stronger. These exercises should include the Arm Curl and Reverse Arm Curl which I mention in the Rotator Cuff section.

Wrist Curl: Stand with your arm by your side. Using a five pound dumbbell, Palm up, bend your wrist slowly upward toward you. Hold this position for ten seconds and then slowly lower the wrist back to the starting position. Repeat curl fifty times, once a day.

Figure 21: Wrist Curl with Palm Facing Forward

Reverse Wrist Curl: Stand with your arm down by your side. Using a five pound dumbbell, Palm down, bend your wrist slowly upward toward you. Hold this position for ten seconds and slowly lower the wrist back to the starting positon. Repeat reverse curl fifty times, once a day.

Figure 22: Reverse Wrist Curl

Un-balanced Wrist Rotation: Extend your arm outward, hold the dumbbell by one knob so that the shaft and the other knob come out on the thumb side of your hand. Try to rotate your wrist so that the other knob rotates to the left, then all the way to the right, and back to center again. Do fifty complete left to right rotations.

Figure 23: Unbalanced Wrist Rotation

Forearm Strengthening Exercises

Roll Up Exercise: Tie a piece of rope about three feet long to the center of a two foot piece of PVC pipe. Hang a five pound weight from the rope. Roll the rope up on the pipe as if it were a spool and then roll it back down. Repeat until tired. The weights can be increased as needed.

Figure 24: Elbow and Wrist Rollup

Elbow and Wrist Flexibility Exercises

Elbow and Wrist Stretch: Hold your wrist with the fingers pointing down toward the floor. Pull down on the wrist until you feel a stretch. Hold this position for fifteen to twenty seconds. Repeat exercise ten times, two times per day.

Figure 25: Elbow and Wrist Stretch

Elbow and Wrist Stretch: Hold your wrist as shown with the fingers pointing away from the floor. Pull the fingers back until you feel a stretch. Hold this position for fifteen to twenty seconds and then slowly return to the starting position. Repeat exercise ten times, two times per day.

Figure 26: Elbow and Wrist Stretch

Ball Squeezing: Hold a soft rubber ball or a soft tennis ball in your hand. Squeeze as hard as you can. Hold this position for fifteen to twenty seconds. Repeat this exercise ten times, two times per day.

Thumb and Fingers Flex: Hook rubber band around the thumb and one finger, and try to close the finger to the palm. Hold for five seconds. Do the same exercise with each of the fingers of the hand twice, two times per day.

Thumb and Fingers Stretch: Start with your palm facing you, hook the rubber band around the thumb and the index finger, and stretch the rubber band between the fingers. Hold for about one second and repeat until tired. You can do this exercise twice, two times per day.

Move the rubber band to each of your other fingers and stretch them individually against the thumb.

Adjacent Fingers Stretch: Put the rubber band across two adjacent fingers and spread them apart, holding for five seconds. Stretch each combination of adjacent fingers in the hand.

Medial epicondylitis is inflammation and pain of the inner side of the elbow where muscles and tendons attach to the bone. The structures involved are the muscles and tendons of the forearm that bring your wrist down as when you flex your wrist. We see this condition in tennis when the timing is off on the forehand stroke and the snapping of the muscle and tendon on the serve. It is caused by repetitive stress and strain to these muscles and tendons and is treated with therapy and rest.

Hand and Wrist Pain

Sore wrists, very common in tennis, may be sprained or sore from overuse. A sprain causes sudden pain and is due to one specific move. An overuse pain comes on gradually and gets progressively worse. The most important thing is to catch it early. Tendinitis can be successfully treated and healed if you get to it early. Icing after tennis will help. So will contrast baths of four or five repetitions of warm water for four minutes, followed by an ice bath of one minute, up to three times a day can be very effective. Make sure you move your hand in warm water. Wearing a splint will rest the tendons and promote healing, and many splints such as a wrist splint help keep the wrist in a comfortable position while sleeping.

Pain at the base of the hand behind the pinky finger may indicate a severe injury. The butt of the racquet continually hitting the hook of the small hamate bone can break the bone. A sports physician will need to take an x-ray to see whether the bone is broken. If it is, it will need to be treated as a fracture. If it is bruised, ice the injury and rest the hand until the pain subsides and use a racquet with a smaller butt. The American player Jonathan Stark suffered this fracture of the hamate when he fell on the court at Roland Garros. He had the surgery performed at Hospital for Special Surgery and with treatment and rehabilitation, he was able to come back and have a good career.

Running to get to the Ball

While working with tennis players all these years I was able to see some great runners. Borg, Gerulaitis, Federer, Chang and Djokovic all possessed great foot speed. This, obviously, enabled them to get to the ball very quickly and it reflected in the great level of their play. Remarkably, they did not suffer many injuries to their legs and feet. Sure, maybe their feet blistered occasionally but nothing that comes to mind with the rest of their lower extremities. With club players it is not the case. There you will see lots of injuries caused by running. In fact, there are more injuries from running than injuries from using your racquet. With club players, I have treated injuries to the foot and ankle, knees, calf, thigh, hamstrings, and back. Many tennis players complain of pain around the kneecap during and after playing.

Recently, when I worked with Pat Cash in Delray Beach, he was still getting knee pain from old injuries. Sudden directional changes can trigger knee pain as well as overuse syndrome conditions. Some say they feel the pain deep in the knee or behind the knee. The pain may come on gradually and the player feels fluid in the knee. These are signs of runner's knee.

You need to see an orthopaedist for an evaluation. Knee injuries are serious and need to be treated. The thigh muscles can be injured when you make a quick stop, usually when you are running with a bent knee. This injury can be treated with ice initially and should be rested. If pain persists, you must see your physician.

Hamstring injuries result often when you have not had a proper warmup and did not spend enough time stretching. The hamstrings are very large and respond to slow and thorough stretching. Regarding recurrent hamstring and quadriceps strains, the following advice is well worth mentioning. Almost without exception, hamstring strains recur because the muscle has never gotten strong enough. It may be flexible, but it's not strong. So, it keeps getting injured. The reason is that tennis players think that they can exercise themselves back into shape after these injuries by doing the same things they always did. If they run, they run again and it's back to the courts, or back to the gym. That's all well and good, but once one of these muscles gets weak, it no longer starts at the same level as your other muscles.

As you exercise, all the muscles get stronger, but you never erase the discrepancy between the injured muscle and the others. So even though your injured hamstring may be stronger than it was when you began, compared to the rest of your body, it's still weak. You must do specific exercises for the specific muscle that was injured. That doesn't mean more exercise, necessarily, it means different exercises. That's why it's vitally important to discover just what it was that went wrong in the first place. You need to find out the mechanism of how it was injured. You need to know "the why". If you don't know what muscle was injured, precisely what muscle, you won't know what muscle to exercise. You just have to be investigative when it comes to taking care of yourself.

Back Stretches and Flexion Exercises

Slow Toe-Touch: While standing, bend you body down to where your head is between your legs. Bend your body down as far as you can, then grab behind your knees, placing your hands behind your knees and try to go a little farther. Hold for ten to fifteen seconds. First begin with three reps and then go up by one every other day until you reach twelve reps.

Figure 27: Back Flexion Slow Toe Touch

Toe-Touch with Rotation: Place your legs apart and bend your body down. Then bend your body with your head going toward your right knee. Stay in that position ten to fifteen seconds. Now come back to the starting position. Bend down again, trying to put your head on your left knee. Stay in that position for ten to fifteen seconds. Begin with three reps and then go up by one every other day until you reach twelve reps.

Figure 28: Back Flexion Slow Toe Touch with Rotation

Hurdler Stretch: Stand up and put one foot on a table. Bend your head toward the table and try to put your head on your knee. Do the same reps as if you were doing the toe touches. Now repeat with other leg.

Figure 29: Hurdler Stretch Standing

Knee Pull with Head Curl: To increase flexibility in the hip, lower back and your buttock muscles. Lie on your back with knees bent and feet flat on the floor. Bring one knee up toward your chest and clasp the knee with both hands. As you pull the knee down gently, curl your head up slightly. Hold for ten to fifteen seconds. Return the leg to the starting position and do the same number of repetitions as for the toe touches. Repeat with the other leg.

Pelvic Tilt: Get on your back, bend your knees, put your feet flat on table, relax the back muscles and tighten your stomach and butt muscles, press your back flat against the table. Your pelvis is tilted forward. When your back is flat, do as many reps as you would do toe touches.

Figure 30: Back Stretch and Flexion (Pelvic Tilt)

Abdominal Curl: Get on your back, with your knees bent your feet flat on the floor, with your hands folded behind your head. Curl your shoulder blades off the floor, with your back on the floor. Hold for five seconds and lower your head and shoulders. Begin with five reps, now increase by five as curls will get less difficult to do.

Figure 31: Back Stretch and Flexion (Abdominal Curl)

Dealing with extension exercises, you will see that the more you exercise the back muscles will lengthen.

Back Extension: You must stand with your arms at your side. Bend backwards while looking up at the ceiling. Stay in that position for ten seconds. Relax and straighten up, returning to your starting position. Extend five more times. Increase by two reps. The more you will do, the less difficult it will be.

Figure 32: Back Extension

Hip Extension: Lie on a table on your back with one leg dangling over the side. Lower the leg from the hip toward the floor. Feel the stretch in your hip, hold for ten seconds. Have your partner push on your knee to increase stretch. Don't let your partner hurt you though! Have them push your knee! Return your leg to the table and repeat the stretch five times. Add stretches two at a time. It will get less difficult.

Figure 33: Back Strengthen Hip Extension

Reverse Sit-up: Your partner has to hold your legs down. Lie face down on a table, with your legs and pelvis on the table. Your partner holds your ankles while you bend at the waist off the edge of the table until your forehead is pointing to the floor. Slowly lift your upper body until it is horizontal again. Do five reps and add two at a time as this becomes easier.

Figure 34: Back Extension/Strengthen Reverse Sit Up

Chapter H: The Shoulder by Todd Ellenbecker

Stresses on the shoulder of the elite tennis player are repetitive and often lead to overuse injury. An understanding of the basic structure and function of the shoulder as well as specific exercises to prevent injury are important for players, coaches, parents and all members of the support team caring for the elite player.

Basic Anatomy and Structure of the Shoulder

The shoulder (glenohumeral joint) is comprised of a ball (head of the humerus) and socket (glenoid) which forms the most mobile joint in the human body. Unlike other joints in the body, the shoulder has very few ligaments and a thin joint capsule providing little overall stability to the joint. The main source of stabilization for the shoulder joint are the muscles.

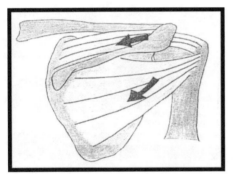

The most important group of muscles which provide stabilization are the rotator cuff muscles. The rotator cuff is made up of 4 muscles. The most common site of injury is not to the actual rotator cuff muscles but rather to its tendons which allow for the attachment of the rotator cuff muscles to the ball (head of the humerus). In addition to providing stability to the shoulder joint, the rotator cuff provides powerful internal rotation (the motion players use to hit a

Figure 35: Back view of the shoulder showing the rotator cuff muscles. Arrows depict the direction the muscle shortens to produce stability and rotation.

forehand and accelerate forward to ball contact on the serve) as well as critically important deceleration following ball contact on the serve. This deceleration or slowing down of the arm is very stressful to the tendon, and is one of the main reasons why the rotator cuff tendons become overloaded and injured with repetitive tennis play.

Characteristics of the Tennis Players Shoulder

Despite the thought that the tennis players dominant arm is much stronger, research studies actually show the rotator cuff muscles (specifically three of the four rotator cuff muscles primarily the ones in the back of the shoulder) to be weaker than the non-tennis playing side. This is likely from the stress during the follow-through of the service motion where the muscle works eccentrically (while it is lengthening). This creates a breakdown and overload to the muscles and their tendons and makes the tennis player's shoulder at risk for injury as a lack of proper strength in these important muscles compromises proper function of the joint.

Figure 36. Amount of external rotation used during the tennis serve in an elite player.

Another adaptation in many tennis players' shoulders is the fact that the arm can be externally rotated very far. This increased flexibility in this direction and the fact that the tennis player's shoulder can be very lax or loose has led to the description of the "Gumby Shoulder" like the rubber cartoon character. Because of this looseness of the shoulder in this backward direction, players and coaches are cautioned against stretching the shoulder forcibly in this direction by placing the arms behind the body. This was a common practice among tennis players and baseball pitchers years ago, but is not recommended.

Despite the ability to rotate the shoulder backward (externally) more than the opposite side, tennis players cannot rotate their shoulders inward very well (internal rotation)

Figure 37. Losing internal rotation likely comes from the

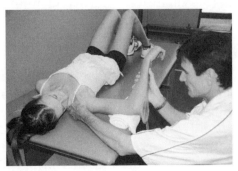

repetitive overuse of the muscles and joint structures and chronic tightness in the back of the shoulder. This loss of internal rotation actually creates harmful movements inside the shoulder and can lead to injury. Having this motion measured by a physical therapist or athletic trainer is important and often leads to the recommendation to perform specific stretches to increase internal rotation range of motion flexibility.

Figure 37: Player having shoulder internal rotation measured. Note how little motion in this direction is available.

Exercises for Prevention of Shoulder Injury

The two most important stretches for the tennis player to perform are the "cross arm" stretch and "sleeper" stretch.

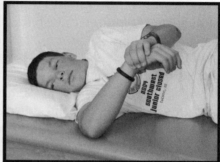

Figure 38: Sleeper Stretch Doing 2-3 repetitions with 20-30 seconds hold during e ach stretch is recommended

To properly perform the cross arm stretch, it is important to stabilize your shoulder blade (scapula) against a wall or stable object to enhance the effectiveness of the stretch. Each of these stretches can be performed both before and especially after tennis play. Research has shown that performance of these stretches either increases or decreases the speed of the tennis serve, however, research also shows that using these stretches as part of a regular program will improve internal rotation range of motion.

In addition to the flexibility changes in the tennis player's shoulder, significant strength adaptations also occur. In the modern game of tennis, 75% of all shots are forehands and serves. During the serve and forehand, powerful internal rotation of the arm occurs which leads to the development of strength in the internal rotators which are located primarily on the front of the body. As mentioned earlier, the muscles in the back of the shoulder while heavily used, are prone to breakdown from the types of muscle work they are being asked to perform. This leads to a weakening of the muscles in the back of the shoulder and shoulder blade area. A muscle imbalance is thereby created. This imbalance in the tennis player's shoulder has been described like having a Porsche sports car in the front of the shoulder and VW Bug in the back of the shoulder. Due to this imbalance, tennis specific exercises emphasize the posterior or back shoulder muscles and shoulder blade or scapular stabilizers to promote balance to the shoulder. Many players and coaches ask, "Doesn't playing tennis simply strengthen these muscles"? The answer is no, research has shown that simply playing tennis does not adequately strengthen the muscles in the back of the shoulder (rotator cuff and scapular stabilizers) that specific exercises are needed to address this need.

Figure 39 shows four exercises that can be used to strengthen the back or posterior part of the rotator cuff. Each of these movement patterns should be performed slowly and with proper form. Amazingly, most young players can only use a 1 pound weight, and even older more experienced players will experience significant muscular fatigue with a 1.5 or 2 pound weight if the exercises are done correctly. Care should be taken to control the weight during both the shortening (raising) and lengthening (lowering) phases of the exercise as this works or prepares the muscle for the specific performance demands encountered during tennis play. Performing these exercises using three sets of 15 to 20 repetitions per set is a good guideline. Increase the weight in ½ pound increments only after you can do all three sets without significant fatigue and without using other parts of your body to compensate. These exercises should not produce pain, just a feeling of burning around the shoulder.

Figure 39: See Below: (sidelying external rotation, shoulder extension, prone horizontal abduction, 90/90 external rotation).

1. SIDELYING EXTERNAL ROTATION:
Lie on uninvolved side, with involved arm at side, with a small pillow between arm and body. Keeping elbow of involved arm bent and fixed to side, raise arm into external rotation. Slowly lower to starting position and repeat.

2. SHOULDER EXTENSION:
Lie on table on stomach, with involved arm hanging straight to the floor. With thumb pointed outward, raise arm straight back into extension toward your hip. Slowly lower arm and repeat.

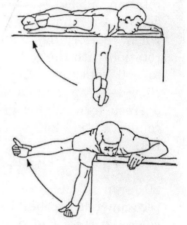

3. PRONE HORIZONTAL ABDUCTION:
Lie on table on stomach, with involved arm hanging straight to the floor. With thumb pointed outward, raise arm out to the side, parallel to the floor. Slowly lower arm, and repeat.

4. 90/90 EXTERNAL ROTATION:
Lie on table on stomach, with shoulder abducted to 90 degrees and arm supported on table, with elbow bent at 90 degrees. Keeping the shoulder and elbow fixed, rotate arm into external rotation, slowly lower to start position, and repeat.

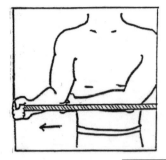

Two other exercises that should be performed using elastic tubing or Thera-band (Hygenic Corp, Akron Ohio, www.thera-bandacademy.com) further assist in providing muscle balance to the tennis players shoulder. External rotation at the side works the back or posterior portion of the rotator cuff as does external rotation at 90 degrees of abduction. Note when performing external rotation with the arm raised to 90 degrees, the arm should be approximately 30 degrees forward for greater comfort and for technical reasons.

Figure 40 & 41 External rotation at side (left photo) & with 90 degrees abduction (below)

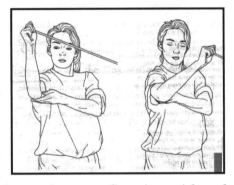

Using three sets of 15 to 20 repetitions is again recommended to build muscular endurance. Starting with red colored tubing is initially recommended with progression to the green color level once the red becomes easy. Avoid using heavy or thick bands or tubing, as these create abnormal loads to the shoulder and encourage compensation from other muscles.

Plyometrics for the Tennis Player's Shoulder

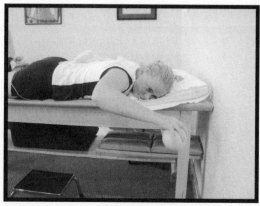

As the player has progressed through the initial strengthening exercises, it is important to progress to exercises that work the muscles at faster speeds and more closely to the manner in which they will be used during actual tennis play. A plyometric exercise is one where a combination of muscle contractions are used to explosively develop muscle power. Specifically, a lengthening or eccentric contraction is followed by a shortening or concentric contraction. In the two exercises listed a small ½ or 1 kilogram medicine ball (1 kg = 2.2 lbs) is used to work the back (posterior) side of the rotator cuff with the arm in the serving position. In the first exercise (figure 42), the player lies on a table and repeatedly drops and quickly catches the ball as fast as possible for 30 second sets. Repeat 2 to 3 times.

Figure 42: 90/90 Prone Plyometric

Remember to do this as quickly as possible. The ball only moves a few inches as you quickly catch and release it as pictured. In the exercise in figure 43, a partner throws the medicine ball slightly in front of the player's hand as they catch and immediately throw the ball forcefully back to the partner. It is important to keep the elbow up (approximately 90 degrees) during this exercise as the ball is initially caught and then forcefully thrown back. Again, multiple sets of 15-20 repetitions are recommended.

Figure 43: 90/90 Reverse toss plyometrics

Role of the Scapula in the Tennis Players Shoulder

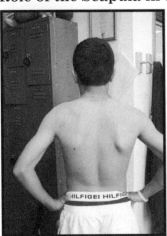

Another area of weakness and vulnerability of the shoulder in the elite tennis player is the shoulder blade or scapula. Changes in shoulder posture also occur in elite tennis players. The dominant shoulder is usually significantly lower, and in the presence of inadequate muscle support often wings or protrudes off the thoracic wall. Prominence of the outline of the shoulder blade or scapula on the dominant side indicates the need for strengthening of several important muscles that stabilize the scapula, most importantly, the serratus anterior and trapezius muscles.

Exercises that are recommended to increase the strength of the scapular stabilizers

> Elite player with right scapular winging.

are the row, external rotation retraction, and the step-up. The row can be performed using elastic resistance or various exercise machines. The key is to ensure that during the row that the shoulder blades are pinched or squeezed together to engage the muscles to a greater extent.

External rotation with retraction involves initially rotating the hands outward, only a few inches, and then pinching the shoulder blades (scapulae) together. It also helps to jut or stick out the chest while squeezing the shoulder blades together. The exercise is repeated for 3 sets of 15 to 20 repetitions.

 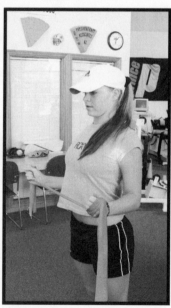

External rotation with retraction exercise: Start position on left and ending position on right photo

The step up is an exercise that uses a 6-8 inch step and involves a rounding out of the back like a cat: at the top phase of the exercise. The exercise is started with the player on their knees, and as strength and core stability develop, the exercise is advanced to performance off the toes like a push up start position. It is important to note, that even though the step-up is a recommended exercise for the scapular stabilizers, it resembles a push-up which is not a recommended exercise for tennis players, as it significantly strains the front of the shoulder. Exercises that stress the shoulders in a position behind the body and load the shoulders in an overhead position are also not recommended. The exercises in this guide specifically address the imbalances and specific needs of tennis players and overhead athletes.

Step-up

Summary

An understanding of the inherent demands on the tennis shoulder as well as the unique adaptations and areas of vulnerability allows players to take the necessary steps to prevent injury and optimize their performance. Application of these exercises and stretches to existing training programs is recommended along with periodic evaluation by a sports medicine professional.

Glossary

Acromioclavicular (AC) Joint

        Joint of the shoulder where acromion process of the scapula and the distal end of the clavicle meet; most shoulder separations occur at this point.

Abduct

        Movement of any extremity away from the midline of the body. This action is achieved by an abductor muscle.

Abrasion

        Any injury which rubs off the surface of the skin.

Adduct

        Movement of an extremity toward the midline of the body. This action is achieved by an adductor muscle.

Adhesion

        Abnormal adherence of collagen fibers to surrounding structures during immobilization following trauma or as a complication of surgery which restricts normal elasticity of the structures involved.

Anabolic Steroids

        Steroids that promote tissue growth by creating protein in an attempt to enhance muscle growth. The main anabolic steroid is testosterone.

Anterior

        The front surface of.

Anterior Compartment Syndrome

> Condition in which swelling within the anterior compartment of the lower leg jeopardizes the viability of muscles, nerves and arteries that serve the foot. In severe cases, emergency surgery is necessary to relieve the swelling and pressure.

Anterior Cruciate Ligament (ACL)

> A primary stabilizing ligament within the center of the knee joint that prevents hyperextension and excessive rotation of the joint. A complete tear of the ACL necessitating reconstruction could require up to 12 month of rehabilitation

Anterior Talofibular Ligament

> A ligament of the ankle that connects the fibula (lateral ankle bone) to the talus. This ligament is often subject to sprain.

Anti-Inflammatory

> Any agent which prevents inflammation, such as aspirin or ibuprofen.

Bruise

> A discoloration of the skin due to an extravasation of blood into the underlying tissues.

Bursa

> A fluid-filled sac that is located in areas where friction is likely to occur, then minimizes the friction; for example between a tendon and bone.

Calcaneofibular Ligament

The ligament that connects the fibula to the Calcaneo bone.

Calf

Large muscle located at the back of the shin that includes the gastrocnemius and the soleus muscles and is responsible for foot plantar flexion and is instrumental in jumping.

Cartilage

Smooth, slippery substance preventing two ends of bones from rubbing together and grating.

Clavicle

The collar bone.

Cold Pack

A pack of natural or synthetic ice that is applied to any injury in order to minimize blood flow in the area to control the injury.

Contusion

An injury to a muscle and tissues caused by a blow from a blunt object.

Dehydration

Loss of body water.

Deltoid Ligament

Ligament that connects the tibia to bones of the medial aspect of the foot and is primarily responsible for stability of the ankle on the medial side. This is sprained less frequently than other ankle ligaments.

Deltoid Muscle

Muscles at top of the arm, just below the shoulder, responsible for shoulder motions to the front, side and back.

Dorsiflexion

Ankle motion such that the foot and toes are moved away from the ground in an upward fashion.

Edema	Accumulation of fluid in organs and tissues of the body; swelling.
Electrolyte	Ionized salts in blood, tissue fluids and cells, including salts of sodium, potassium and chlorine.
Electrolyte Drink	Fluid for replacing electrolytes, such as Gatorade Thirst Quencher or Powerade.
Epicondylitis	Inflammation in the elbow due to overuse.
Eversion	Action of the ankle turning outward.
Extension	Action of straightening of a joint as achieved by an extensor muscle.
External Rotation	Lateral movement of a joint or extremity to the outside.
Fascia	A connective tissue sheath consisting of fibrous tissue and fat which unites the skin to the underlying tissue.
Femur	Thigh bone; longest bone in the body.
Fibula	Smaller of the two bones in the lower leg; runs from the knee to the ankle along the outside of the lower leg.
Flexibility	The ability of muscles to relax and yield to stretch forces.
Flexibility Exercises	General term used to describe exercise performed by an athlete to passively or actively elongate soft tissue without the assistance of another person.
Flexion	Motion of bending a joint as achieved by a flexor muscle.

Fracture	Breach in continuity of a bone. Types of fracture include simple, compound, comminuted, greenstick, incomplete, impacted, longitudinal, oblique, stress or transverse.
Hammer Toe	Condition when the first digit of a toe is at a different angle than the remaining digits of the same toe.
Hamstring	Category of muscle that runs from the buttocks to the knee along the back of the thigh. It functions to flex the knee, and is oft times injured as a result of improper conditioning or lack of muscle flexibility.
Illiotibial Band	A thick, wide fascial layer that runs from the iliac crest to the knee joint and is occasionally inflamed as a result of excessive running.
Internal Rotation	Rotation of a joint or extremity medially, to the the inside.
Inversion	Action of the ankle turning inward.
Ligament	Band of fibrous tissue that connects bone to bone or bone to cartilage and supports and strengthens joints.

Magnetic Resonance Imaging (MRI)

> Imaging procedure in which a radio frequency pulse causes certain electrical elements of the injured tissue to react to this pulse. Through this process a computer display and permanent film establish a visual image. MRI does not require radiation and it very useful in the diagnosis of soft tissue, disc, and meniscus injuries.

Metatarsals

> Five long bones of the foot, running from the ankle to the toes.

Morton's Neuroma

> Involves the nerves and is usually the result of a trauma to the foot, causing inflammation and sharp pain, usually between the third and fourth toes.

Morton's Toe

> A hereditary condition in which the second toe is longer than the first toe. This can cause mechanical imbalances which produce pain with weight bearing.

Neuritis

> Inflammation of a nerve.

Orthotic

> Any device applied to or around the body in the care of physical impairment or disability, commonly used to control foot mechanics.

Phalanx

> Any bone of the fingers or toes; plural is phalanges.

Plantar

> Pertaining to the sole of the foot.

Plantar Fascia

> The tight band of muscle beneath the arch of the foot.

Plantar flexion

Ankle motion such that the toes are pointed toward the ground.

Pronation

In the foot, it is a combination of motions resulting in a position such that the foot is abducted and everted. Foot pronation can be a by-product of an arch problem, leg length discrepancy, or chronically bad running mechanics; can be compromised with the use of an orthotic. In the hand, pronation is movement of the forearm into the palm down position.

Proximal

Near the source, nearest any point being described. The elbow is proximal to the hand.

Rotator Cuff

Comprised of four muscles in the shoulder area that can be irritated by overuse. The muscles are the supraspinatus (most commonly injured), infraspinatus, teres minor, and subscapularis.

Rotator Cuff Impingement Syndrome

A microtrauma or overuse injury caused by stress. The four stages are: 1) tendinitis with temporary thickening of the bursa and rotator cuff, 2) fiber dissociation in the tendon with permanent thickening of the bursa and scar formation, 3) A partial rotator cuff tear of less than 1 cm, and 4) a complete tear of 1 cm or more.

Shin Splint	A catch-all syndrome describing pain in the shin that is not a fracture or tumor and cannot be defined otherwise.
Supination	Movement of the forearm into a palm-up position.
Synovial Fluid	Lubricating fluid for joints and tendons, produced in synovium, or the inner lining of a joint.
Synovitis	Inflammation of the synovial lining of a joint.
Talus	The ankle bone that articulates with the tibia and fibula to form the ankle joint.
Tendinitis	Inflammation of the tendon and/or tendon sheath, caused by chronic overuse or sudden injury.
Tendon	Tissue that connects muscle to bone.